GEMS OF TIME

LESLEY CORTE

GEMS OF TIME

PAST LIVES

WITH
MYSTERY, ROMANCE,
AND SPIRIT GUIDES

in·fluence
PARTNERS IN PUBLISHING

Published by Corte Press
2088 Line 12 North, Oro-Medonte, Ontario L0L 1T0 Canada
in partnership with Influence Publishing Inc., February 2024
ISBN 978-1-7381741-0-2

Copyediting: Erin Della Mattia
Proofreading: Lee Robinson
Cover Design: Andrew Croft
Typesetting: Tara Eymundson

DISCLAIMERS: Readers of this publication agree that neither the author nor their publisher will be held responsible or liable for damages that may be alleged as resulting directly or indirectly from the use of this publication. Neither the publisher nor the author can be held accountable for the information provided by, or actions resulting from, accessing these resources.

While all the stories in this book are true, some names and identifying details have been changed to protect the privacy of the people involved.

For Jim

My darling husband,

my partner on earth and in spirit

CONTENTS

Part III - STARSHIP

ACKNOWLEDGMENTS

When I began this process of writing, I had no idea what new things I was about to learn. I give great thanks to all the people who led me on this journey, especially my brilliant and very patient editor, Erin Della Mattia, who has tuned up my writing extensively and buoyed me when uncertainty crept into my thoughts.

Thank you to Julie Ann, the founder of Influence Publishing, for her enthusiasm and help in fleshing out the initial gem of an idea to write a book about past lives. It took me five years to put my ideas about life on "Starship Earth" on paper, and Julie's input was an essential part of the structure and flow of the stories which make up this book.

All the people at Influence Publishing have been helpful in guiding this process along, prodding me where needed and encouraging me to continue writing through to the end.

I'm so appreciative of the input from regressionist Garnet Schulhauser and mystical medium Ara Parisien, both of whom are writers themselves. Garnet's suggestion that I might have writers in spirit assist me opened up a channel for the poetry that fell onto the page. Ara's suggestion to let it flow helped get over the inevitable writer's block, and her insightful and positive readings helped clarify my direction.

I am thankful to the small group of women whom I met through a breakout session on Hay House writer's workshops — Julie, Denise, Jennifer, Julanne, Margo, Lucy, and Diana. We have had great fun encouraging and challenging one another to finish and publish our books — each one a different take on healing — during our weekly Zoom sessions. It is so wonderful to share this experience with a group of highly intelligent and spirited women.

Thank you to my dear friend Gail Mcbride who hung in with me during the writing of this book and helped steady my course. Thank you also to my creative and talented friend Shelley Silverman who put up with my many changes of mind and injected much-needed humor when I became too serious. I couldn't have done it without both of your support.

Thank you to my darling friend Lesley Finlayson who gave her unconditional support during the emotional ups and downs of life and death that I write about in this book. I am also grateful for the many other friends, too numerous to name, who have been part of the Spirit Family I traveled with through this lifetime. We made it interesting, didn't we!

I send much love and appreciation to my family for the love they share with me. I am learning how valuable and rare it is to have such a caring group of people as support.

I must also share the joy I feel for the next generation — the nieces and nephew and their partners who have followed their own stars. You have restored my faith in humanity and have given me hope for the future of life on this planet.

And of course, I have to thank my husband Jim for the profound love, adventures, challenges, and depth of Spirit we have shared during the many years we journeyed together.

INTRODUCTION

This book has been in me for centuries. It has been written in the cells of my body, in the DNA of hopes and dreams, in fighting the good fight on Earth and in the stars.

It was written at a time when I felt a powerful urge to express the true beliefs about life that I have kept silent for so long.

In my early thirties, working for years as a graphic artist and designer, trusting in my intuition and the visual imagery that easily dropped into my head, I knew that I needed to stretch and go deeper into the inner workings of my mind. At the beginning of my spiritual quest, I kept my thoughts for a select group of people — fellow questioners — hiding my true feelings from the greater world.

For so long, I have been afraid to expose my inner life for fear of reprisals from family, friends, and strangers alike.

Despite knowing of many successful psychic and spiritual people who have become accepted by the world, I had a deep-seated fear of exposing myself to criticism. Some unknown negative consequences were sure to occur. Fear held me back for years.

But fear can be a great motivator. As can curiosity. I have both. By exploring my inner world, I reconnected with memories of my current life as well as past lifetimes which helped to explain what kept my self-expression bottled up. I have also seen myself in other roles in other lifetimes with many of the people I am closest to today. This brought even greater clarity to the role I was meant to play in my current life.

I am part of a generation exploring the idea of the coming of the Age of Aquarius. Many times, astrologers have told me my chart reveals that I have Mercury in Aquarius, which indicates that I will be in the media. Such a prediction didn't seem attainable to the shy, introverted young woman I was.

The Aquarian Age is now upon us. The Grand Conjunction of Jupiter and Saturn that occurred in December 2020 took place in Aquarius, the sign of innovation and visions for the future. This was the first time Jupiter and Saturn met in Aquarius since 1405, when their meeting heralded in the Renaissance. This tells us that, just like in 1405, something in the zeitgeist is at work in the world today. We are experiencing rapid change in many aspects of our societal structures.

A spark of something new was ignited in me that awakened me to a dream one night.

I was at a center that helped feed people in need, in a room like a wide corridor with rows of desks, two per row, leading far back into the distance. They were wooden school desks like the ones I sat at in elementary school, initials with "_____ was here" carved into the surface. In the front row was a man who looked like Obama who told me he was working with Princeton. A woman I was somehow associated with had ushered me in to see him and then left. The man asked me to work with him as an understudy. He was a lawyer. I was a lawyer too.

I wasn't sure if I knew the law enough but, as I focused, my mind opened up into a field of wisdom ...... Aha! ...... The laws of the universe. So, I knew what the dream was about ......

I had been requested by the Prince of Soul, the Prince of the Laws of the Universe, to begin to work with the higher levels again in a more organized fashion — to write a book.

The idea to write a book, which was previously filed under "maybe in the future," re-emerged. It felt like the right time.

And so this book came into being. It is a collaboration between me, my personal spirit guide, and other magnificent, beneficent spirit guides, some with whom I have intimate relationships and some I met while writing. Miraculously I attracted the voices of writers who have passed, interested in this joint venture. I am completely intrigued by what they have had to say, their spirit energy funneling down to me to spill out as words on a page.

The man I called my husband in this life also returned to me in spirit and wrote with me. He presented himself on my meditation table as the Emperor card from the Thoth tarot deck. It is a beautiful card of orange and yellow imparting great energy and strength. My husband's spirit continues to follow my progress and bolsters my energy to bring forth the source story that really began with our connection together.

Each one of us has the ability to draw from the universe all the wisdom and assistance we need to fulfill our unique talents and purposes in order to shine in our true magnificence. This truth is the essence of this book.

I
ROMANCE

SANDS OF TIME

The sands of time blow off the cliff as dust

Float through the air in mist of moments past

And florid scenes of hope and dreams are dashed

The lovely rose hides its secrets within its scent

The home of spirit is found within the time spent

Worlds within worlds roiling, tossing, turning,

Momentum churning of instinct and intellect.

Moments of power and intensity

Moments of love and lightness

Moments to reconnect and make whole again

Rolling home.

1

THE GREAT ESCAPE

The outline of the imposing temple looms against the setting sun, projecting shadows across the sands that stretch towards the horizon, signaling the path forward. I swiftly leave the perfumed scent of the temple to breath in the dirt-dry air as I fly down the steps.

Fear propels me. The pounding in my chest magnifies the need to speed forward. I turn my head back to see the man who is my lover in the distance. I have no time for goodbyes. I run. My legs carry me towards the horizon where I will meet up with others.

The vision slowly fades into the mists of time. I am left wondering why it was so urgent that I leave the mystical life of the Egyptian temple behind. Somehow I know that I had incurred the wrath of the high priest. What had I done? What propels me forward into the unknown?

Had there been sexual indiscretions that precipitated my ouster?

These questions have swirled around this scene many times in my mind. The mystery has run as an undercurrent in my life for years. I needed to solve it but had no idea how …

But the query is overshadowed by the first glimpse of dreamy blue eyes.

Now, here is a man standing at my front door whom I had recently spoken to on the phone, waiting to pick up the table saw from the workshop of my deceased husband. And he was the lover I had left behind as I ran from the temple!

"Hi, I'm Leo," he said.

But I am getting way ahead of myself. Let me explain ……

I am on a quest to discover what really happened to me in that lifetime in Egypt which I have envisioned many times before. I'll start by tracing this back to my first glimpse of a past life in Egypt.

A Power Connection

Many years earlier, as a twenty-four-year-old, I was sitting in the house of my good friend Bernadette with my new-found love Jim. Bernadette was leading a past life regression for us. Jim and I sat opposite each other with our eyes closed. Bernadette led us into a light trance, then asked us what we were seeing. A vision came up immediately. I saw myself high up on top of a golden-colored hill. There was no vegetation, only rocks overlooking a valley far below.

"Come back to reality." I slowly opened my eyes to Jim, my swarthy new man with intense brown eyes and a mass of Mediterranean curls. He told me he was at the bottom of a hill, looking up at me longingly, knowing he could never touch me as he wished to do.

"I was feeling the bitterness that comes with unrequited love," he said. We were all surprised that Jim and I envisioned the same scene.

In that moment, I was an Egyptian princess. In that moment, he was a laborer, a builder of the pyramids. This past life experience was confirmed as we celebrated our first Christmas together. Jim and I poured over a large book about the building of the pyramids, the energy of an Egyptian lifetime seeping into my bones. It was the powerful beginning of a truly magnificent connection.

It seems that my friend Bernadette had nudged the chemistry between Jim and me with her interest in the occult. She was also the person who introduced me to a lifetime journey of exploring spirit.

I MEET THE SAMURAI GENERAL

Jim was the man for me. In the beginning, I knew him as the tool man in the closet. I had seen him many times going in and out of the tool closet while hanging art for a show at a small Victoria art college in which I was taking a photography class. When I heard he had broken up with his girlfriend, the receptionist there, I told myself that the next party I saw him at, he would be mine.

A Halloween party provided the perfect setting. I went as a cat on the prowl, with little mice hanging off my belt and a papier-mâché cat head I had made myself. The head quickly came off so I could stalk my prey more easily. Wandering into the kitchen, I encountered a silver-faced man in tights, a Japanese kimono, and high-heeled sponge flip-flops with *tabi* socks — the ones with a separate big toe. Jim became my samurai warrior. Over the years of our marriage, I had visions of the many past lifetimes we had spent together, including the one in Egypt where another man turned out to be more significant. But that comes much later.

The samurai lifetime surfaced several times. At the start of our relationship, Jim introduced me to the director Akira Kurosawa, whose films we watched at the local university. Jim was enamored with the actor Toshiro Mifune, who played the lead in many of the films. Jim resembled him in face and stature, and as we began to frequent a Japanese restaurant, I introduced him to the chef as Mr. Mifune. From then on, he was the Japanese actor when we went out for sushi. Jim shared this Japanese obsession with a friend, and they started to call each other Jim-san and Bill-san. I began to understand the social structure of feudal Japan as I read the James Clavell book *Shogun.* The idea of hara-kiri turned my stomach — pun intended. Only later did I learn the true import of our joint interest in this culture.

One evening as we sat in a café, me between Jim and another good male friend, a Japanese scene flashed in my mind. I was a geisha to these two samurai generals. It was a stunning experience — the first time I had spontaneously experienced a past life.

I had to interrupt the conversation. "Guys, I have to tell you what I just saw!"

I told them I had just seen them as samurai generals discussing their political ambitions together. I was there to entertain them, serving them sake in small ceramic cups. Equally strong and tall, these two men had the presence of generals. Years later, I learned that there had been some tension between them over my affections. The vision made sense.

A Military Man

Getting to know Jim as a person beyond the tool man in the closet, he told me about his stint in the US Navy. "What?" I thought. "I'm dating a military guy? Who signs up for the military? No one I know in my generation."

But Jim was ten years older than me and had joined what was called the "kiddie cruise" in the US military. If you signed up at seventeen, you could serve for only three years. It was at a time before the Vietnam War had produced the first wave of anti-war protests in the country, the beginning of foment for peace. We're still working on that now! Not doing so well! But back then, the Navy was a way for Jim to escape the small-town mentality of the big city of Houston and begin to experience a wider world.

On our walks, Jim was drawn to a particular point of land that jetted out into the Strait of Juan de Fuca, which he told me reminded him of being on the bow of a ship. He explained to me what life was like on an aircraft carrier in the South Pacific. The bunks were about two feet apart and stacked four high — pretty stifling. To escape the feeling of confinement, brave souls would lie at night on the edge of the bow, floating in a field of stars. It was dangerous. Some sailors slipped over the edge into the blackness of the Pacific, never to be seen again.

Jim was a munitions officer — another red flag. "Who *is* this guy?" He was loading bombs onto planes when I was still in Grade 1. Explaining the dangers on the carrier he told me, "Planes would take off fully loaded and returned void of weapons — America's secret bombing of Laos."

Jim's favorite place in the South Pacific was Japan. No surprise to me. After all, I had met up with him in a Japanese costume, maybe not so much costume but persona. Jim had escaped the Vietnam War by less than two months. He escaped towards freedom. Los Angeles gave him permission to reinvent himself. He became a surfer dude. I met the guy who finally became an artist and a builder.

WHAT HAPPENED?
The first Christmas Jim and I spent together was also the first Christmas I didn't spend with my family in Toronto since moving to

the West Coast after university. We had become that close. So, it was a complete shock when Jim broke it off in January. I was heartbroken. Perhaps requited love was too much for him. He liked the pursuit. But I was the one doing the pursuing.

I did pursue him again a few months later. A Lina Wertmüller film festival was playing at our local theatre. We had seen her other films together, but not *Swept Away*. I knew that Jim would be there. I walked into the theatre, sparsely populated by foreign-film enthusiasts. Jim's tall figure stood out, and I slid into the seat next to him. Had I known that this was the sexiest film that I could have chosen? No. But as a prelude to reignite Jim's passion for me, it did the trick. We moved into a rented home together shortly after this fortuitous reunion ......

Next on Jim's agenda was buying a house of our own. This signaled a deeper commitment to our relationship, and I was very happy to go along with the idea.

During the early period of our reunion, we were both working as graphic artists, supporting each other and sharing design ideas. This included renovating the 1911 Victorian-style house we bought, with the stained-glass windows and terrible linoleum tiles. Our world became one of drawing, typefaces and layout, scraping glue off old fir floors, breaking through lath and plaster, replacing walls, and spiritual explorations. Children were in my sights but not immediately.

Around this time, I joined a psychic development class — Kitty's class. The term "psychic" has now become outré for it gives off a shady vibe, but it truly is spiritual development. We always ask for the highest and the best when initiating the mind/spirit quest, as our teacher recommended.

I originally went to see this little lady with an English accent for a psychic reading. The contents of the reading are long gone from my memory, but the invitation to join her class remains. She seemed hesitant, at first, to invite me, but something she was picking up from the ether told her I should be there. I later discovered several past lives in which we had known each other.

I hadn't yet realized that I was psychic, but I was interested in her class partly due to all the Jane Roberts books I had read, with the channeled messages from her spirit friend Seth who brought forth such amazing information. The class began with an exercise in psychometry, the practice of holding an object and tuning into the energy it carries. Without knowing whose object I was holding, I experienced visions that resonated with the owner. It became clear that it was easy for me to tune in to the energy. I didn't know where the images or words were coming from, but I was hooked ......

* * *

"Marriage? Hmmm … I'm not sure."

For the next few years, Jim and I lived together, but I was having doubts about making a commitment. A vision of myself in Persia during a guided meditation wowed me and gave me the insight I needed.

I found myself in an exotic courtyard garden surrounded by stone walls with a trickling fountain in the center. Seated on a stone bench, I was in a passionate embrace with my lover. I knew this was forbidden. If discovered, I would be put to death by my sheik, who happened to be … Jim! And my lover … my grade-twelve boyfriend! Hello again! I had pined for this beautiful, flawed boy/man when I first left home for university, and even as an adult I still had dreams about him. I was stunned. Now I understood. I was holding on to my younger self in a past relationship and resisting taking responsibility for making a mature decision for my future. This revelation helped me make the choice — Jim and I were married not long after buying our first house together.

CHAKRA HEALING

The following year, I attended a psychic fair in the Crystal Gardens, a fitting location with its soaring domed ceilings of glass. I was casually walking past booths, trying to decide which one to stop at, when someone interrupted my thoughts.

"You are thinking that they do not know who you are."

I stopped short. In front of me was a handsome man with crystal blue eyes and a shock of dark, curly hair. He stood next to a small booth with a massage table.

"What?" was all I could muster. What a strange pronouncement coming from a stranger. I had no idea what he was talking about, but I was drawn in and lay down on the table.

The man placed a series of brass Tibetan bowls along my body, the largest one on my lower belly and the smallest on my third eye and above my head. He then made them sing, turning a wand around each one — my first introduction to chakra healing.

I still didn't understand the implication of the initial statement that drew me into his orbit. There was a magic about Akim the healer that kept me intrigued over a period of a couple of years. At one point, Akim intimated that we might work together. His magnetism attracted me, but this would have meant upending my entire life. And I realized that he would be the leader, I would be his assistant. Something in me told me I had to be my own star.

As I got to know him, Akim revealed to me that we had known each other in ancient Egypt and that we both had needed to escape. That was the first time I'd heard about this. For some reason, I didn't ask him why we had to run, and we lost touch before I broached the subject again. Yet, the escape from the temple became the strand, the vision that would resurface several times over the course of my life. Perhaps I was meant to discover the answer myself.

Years after meeting Akim, the scene of running down the temple steps again flashed in front of my eyes during a guided meditation. It was very clear to me that it had some sexual connotation, but what had actually happened was still a mystery. It took many years to unravel the circumstances surrounding it. In the meantime, I was living the life of my dreams with Jim.

In My Heart of Hearts

The World Exposition came to Vancouver. Jim and I had a profound experience touring the Egyptian pavilion at Expo 86. Entering through a colonnade of towering golden columns, we stepped into a dimly lit chamber that emanated an other-worldly aura. The sarcophagus of Ramses II rested on a giant dais, holding sway with its power. Instantly, chills ran through my entire body … I had been a daughter of Ramses II. I just *knew* that I had been his daughter, one of the many born by the women of his harem.

After this awareness, visions of Egypt began to appear during my meditations. I floated down the Nile in the sultry heat as a princess, my servants fanning me with palm fronds as the royal barque was propelled forward by yet more servants. Years later, I was mesmerized while reading Elisabeth Haich's autobiography *Initiation* in which she recalls a lifetime spent training as a priestess in a temple in Egypt. From reading her book, I learned that the priests had an understanding of energy vibration on many levels, visible and invisible. I again just knew that I too had trained as a priestess in the temple. The book inspired my own awareness of my ancient knowledge as the intriguing idea that sound was used to move stone came to me in a deep meditation ......

As these thoughts became part of my understanding of myself, I began to dream of living in a part of the world with palm trees and sunshine. Many years would go by until this dream re-emerged as very important to my life's work.

INVITATION TO REFLECT

As a young adult searching for a relationship that would last, I took a leap of faith and followed my friend's interest in mysticism to go deeper into the inner workings of the mind. By confirming my connection to Jim, my first past life regression proved to be a nexus point that directed my entire wonder-filled life.

My friend Bernadette introduced me to the writings of Jane Roberts, and I was hooked on the insights from her spirit guide, Seth. I enhanced my own explorations by creating a special spot in my house, a red swan chair placed next to a window in my bedroom. Each day I would be drawn to sit and contemplate my many questions, and I found that, if I trusted the answers that came to me, my life ran more smoothly and things seemed to work out as I had hoped.

Q. In what areas of your life do you wish you had more clarity? Would you like to have more insight into parts of your life that do not seem easy, parts that you wonder about? Do you want more understanding regarding a problem? Do you want more understanding about your relationships or why you chose to be with a certain spouse or lover?

Can you find or create a space in which you can peacefully contemplate and meditate on your questions? What might this space look like?

2

SPIRITS ABOUND

My body is a gift, enabling me to ground my spiritual journey within the illusion of time and space. It is neither my ultimate reality nor my true identity. I use the body as it was meant to be used — as a vessel through which to express my love.

— Marianne Williamson

"How could you do this to me?! I love you. How could you treat me this way?" I cry out in disbelief as I watch the priest turn his back on me and walk away. He seems to feel nothing about what had just transpired. We had engaged in "the devil's work" according to the Catholic Church, and I am left devastated. The baby I just birthed is whisked away, never to be seen again by me. I know what its fate will be. My sister nuns have rejected me for my indiscretions. I know they are secretly envious of this forbidden love affair. But I never anticipated that the father would reject me as well. We knew that the love between a man and a woman is divine, yet he is choosing the dictates of the Church over his love for me.

Deep in the background, a voice intoned, "Gently begin to bring yourselves back into the room."

As I slowly opened my eyes and left my reality, I was confronted with another world ...... "What? Where am I?" ...... I found myself seated in a circle of friends, unsure if this was reality or an illusion. Was Jim really the man I was in love with? I blinked in disbelief that the room was real. I had felt so alive in the vision I had just experienced that it took a few minutes to fully inhabit my body in the twentieth century. A guided meditation had landed me in what felt like France in the 1880s, maybe earlier. I had met my spirit guide. His name was Jonas. And I was furious with him.

After sharing my vision with the group, someone told me that recently graveyards had been discovered in France that revealed many infant skeletons. It confirmed to me that what I had seen in my mind had been a true experience in a past life.

I was at the stage of my life when my hormones were loudly proclaiming "It's time to have a baby." And in my mind's eye I saw my grandmother, Nannan, being born to me. I was ready. But nothing came of it. Had I carried a fear of pregnancy into this life? Perhaps my mother's watchful eye on me through my teen years had somehow been karmic, the price I had to pay for my indiscretions in a past life.

I have been in psychic contact with Jonas since my vision of my life as a nun in France. He alerts me to his presence with a purple flash in the upper corner of my left eye. When that flashes, I know he is there. He can be quite persistent if he has something important to tell me. Intellectually I know he's with me all the time. In meditation he will say to me, "Mention my name." As I do, I'm taken deeper. He sends me prayers, suggestions for the day, visions, potentials for the future. And he loves to lecture on topics of history. All these things come to me in my meditations and also in odd moments of the day. All people who meditate can access such wisdom if they can let go of their rational mind and allow the insights to come to them.

Vows

After my first contact with Jonas, I had the realization: "Jonas, we made a vow. I would return and you would be with me in spirit."

The intensity of love I had experienced for this man in my vision of the convent gave me a new outlook on my present life and my present man. I don't believe there is just one soulmate for each of us, but many options for deep connection in partnership.

An experience I had one late night confirmed this for me. I had gone to bed before my husband. As I was drifting off to sleep, Jim walked past my side of the bed. Coming back through the layers of consciousness, I opened my eyes and thought "So *this* is the man I chose to be with," as if I was dropping in from another planet.

WENDY

I met Wendy soon after joining the psychic circle of my spiritual teacher, Kitty Massey. Wendy came to me, in a meditation, as a bright yellow spark in the southeast corner of my eye. She called herself Wendy. I thought this was a strange name for a spirit guide. It seemed too earthly and not very wise-sounding — more appropriate for a child.

At the time, she told me: "I am part of the welcoming committee, Lesley. I am your guide through the steps into your new life. Challenges will be overcome. Obstructions will be knocked down rapidly. We will give you all the necessary processes, steps to take. I will come to you when major changes are occurring in your life,"

"OK," I said to myself. "I guess she's here to help me overcome the hesitations and thoughts that creep into my thinking." I needed help with the negative judgments that ran through my head as if hearing them from my mother. All my childhood training had left me distrustful of my own beliefs and intuition.

"Now," said Wendy, "a quick lesson in overcoming negative thoughts. It's called one-two-three snap. Any time a negative thought comes into your head, say 'one-two-three SNAP.' This is a pattern interrupt that can take your mind from one idea to another in an instant."

Wendy knows me well — that I have a Cinderella complex from childhood, when I felt like the chief cook and bottle washer in my home while my mother played at her special activities. Whether she was in her flower gardens fussing with her peonies or in her sewing room surrounded by shelves of fabric lengths awaiting a pattern, I helped create the perception that she was a great housekeeper for my father's arrival home from work. I have had to break through a lingering feeling of resentment every time I set about to clean or tidy my house. The resentment took root early in my tweens as I wielded a vacuum wand like a golf club around the living room. If the coffee table had been an Italian molded glass table, like I own now, instead of Scandinavian teak, there would surely have been divots of sparkling glass scattered on the Chinese rug. Wendy knows that I battle with this demon of resentment daily. While it has diminished over the years, I still need to be reminded that cleaning up my desk frees my mind to start with a blank slate.

It must have been at that point as a teenager that I unconsciously vowed that I wouldn't become "just a housekeeper." The comedian Roseanne Barr renamed it "Domestic Goddess" — I say "slave to the material world." Jim and I agreed on that point, equally contributing to housework as we were both more absorbed in our creative work lives.

Housework. Does God really care if I make my bed?

THE BELLS

I was introduced to The Bells much later, and you will hear more about them as this story opens up. During a personal meditation, they gave me a quick and tantalizing description of the group and how they are represented in the world. I was intrigued and wanted more.

The Bells speak to me as an undifferentiated group. "You, Lesley, have been interspersed throughout history with other emissaries of The Bells. There are twelve of you emissaries this time on the planet Earth. One is in Belarus. Two are in England, one in France, one in Germany, one in Mexico, one in China, one in India, one in Nepal, and of course you in Canada." The last two were not named. "The United States is void of any Bells at this time because the ultimate masculine power is being abused within the country. The rest of you around the world are working to change this. You are bringing your energy through to change this dynamic, and that is why you are cheering any aggression against the United States president (Trump) at this time — just diminishment of his power. Donald Trump is not the reincarnation of Hitler, but he is closely connected to Hitler's authoritarian role in Germany in the early- to mid-1900s."

Several years later, a message came from The Bells. "Belarus, Belarus, Belarus, Belarus ……"

"Belarus keeps popping in," I acknowledged.

"Take a look on your map. It will be a major flashpoint of power in the world. You will not have a world war as the Second World War."

While writing this book, I reread this prediction and was shocked at how prescient the information was. Russia had initiated its invasion of Ukraine from Belarus.

I am part of an interesting soul group of spirits! They have much to say about what I write and are constantly surprising me with new understanding.

INVITATION TO MEET YOUR GUIDE

We are never really alone. Each one of us has a guide or guides — you may call them guardian angels. These beings follow our earthly lives and are there to give us guidance and love. I was completely unaware of the existence of spirit guides until I was led by my teacher to meet mine. As I describe, it was a "wow" experience. Little did I know that these spirits would be the objective observers to guide my life. I thank them every day for their assistance with everything, big and small. I have truly lived a life with spirit.

Q. Did you have an invisible friend when you were a child? If so, you are fortunate to have met one of your spirit guides.

If you want to meet your guides, invite them in. You can do so by sitting quietly, focusing on your breath, and opening your mind. Then ask, "What is your name?"

You may be surprised by the first thing that comes to you. Don't judge what happens.

OR

If nothing comes to you, you can use your sleep mode to answer. As you sleep, your rational mind is out of the way — this allows your intuition complete freedom. I like to keep a small notebook next to my bed in which I write questions for my mind to ponder as I sleep.

You can write or just ask the question "Who is my Spirit Guide?" before you go to sleep. In the morning, allow yourself to wake up slowly, paying attention to what filters through your mind before you have reached full waking consciousness.

This is a great technique to answer *any* question or resolve *any* dilemma.

3

I CHOSE MY FAMILY?

*Lots of things don't make sense at first, when only the physical
senses are used. What does your heart say?*
— Mike Dooley, *Notes from the Universe*

On a sunny Saturday afternoon in a suburb of Toronto, my nine-year-old self sat at the dining room table with my family eating hot dogs for lunch. I have no idea what the conversation was about, but I do remember a small snippet. I announced, "I think going to church is a waste of time."

My father responded, "If you ever say that again, I will beat you within an inch of your life."

This was certainly my most chilling experience of being told to be quiet. Phrases like "you're only talking to hear yourself talk" were common in my younger years. This message stuck in my subconscious mind, to resurface as I developed my psychic abilities many years later. I became very cautious about sharing my abilities with anyone who I thought might respond negatively, especially my family. So, I kept it under wraps until I finally knew that it was the only real issue left for me to deal with in my life. The messages I was receiving from the spirits were meant to be shared.

As a result of stifling my voice, I became shy, particularly as my family began to move to a new city — and thus me to a new school — every year or two. It affected my life adversely for a long time. Speaking out ' twas not meant to be for Lesley. And yet, as a nine-year-old, I did have a very clear opinion on matters of spirit.

My father's anger was not often turned on me. In fact, he was my best pal as a young girl. I remember fondly watching him on Saturdays as he labored at his basement work bench, building things for the house. I remember him taking me to the barber shop when I was five and sitting in the chair next to him as he had his hair cut by his barber and I had my hair cut by my barber, Walter, who gave me a cute pixie cut. I remember going for walks with my father in the woods that bordered our part of the Don Mills suburb, picking wild-flowers and returning home to look them up in the wildflower book he had bought me. Being the most supportive of my two parents, I couldn't afford to lose his love, so I became a good girl, behaving myself as I was told.

I have seen visions of a lifetime that I lived with my father, John Davies, when he was a patrician, one of the political leaders in ancient Rome. I was his wife, and we lived in a beautiful compound, an extravagant home with a courtyard in the middle. I know I came into this family to be with my father again in my current lifetime.

Jonas joined in: "Of course you were meant to be with your father. He is part of your soul family and loves you dearly."

JONAS ABOUT DAD

As I was working on this book, I sometimes re-experienced the thoughts and feelings of these moments from my childhood. I felt the emotional effects in my body and often needed to stretch and move more to relieve the discomfort.

One morning as I sat to meditate, I asked for healing. Jonas responded: "The weakness in your back is being healed. You cannot propel yourself through the emotional miasma without some distress and discouragement that relates to your early childhood."

"That makes me feel better. I don't have to pretend to be perfect."

Jonas continued: "So, you know you were meant to be with your father — this man with the middle name 'Whately' — for the purposes of connecting in spirit. You noted that one of your relatives, Bishop Whately, wrote one of the hymns in the *Book of Hymns*. This side of the family had a great affinity for the Church. Now, your father put himself in service of this Church as the accountant, which was his vocation. You yourself, at a young age, knew that the strictures of the Church were faulty representations of the true message of Jesus, and yet you learned much about your culture through attending the services and Sunday school. Also, you gained the understanding of the need to meet and greet each other. The Church of England was your spiritual kindergarten. But you and others of the boomer generation imagined for yourselves a greater freedom of behavior and understanding of the word of Jesus, the word of God, the word of Spirit. Your generation expressed this in new ways. Words of great import came through theatre and music. *Jesus Christ Superstar*, *Hair*'s dawning of the Age of Aquarius, and the power of 'peace and love' were all a modernization of the message."

Death of a Father

The phone rang one Sunday morning as I was racing around the house, booking a quick flight and packing a bag, about to fly off to Houston to meet Jim. He had gone ahead to say his goodbyes to his stepfather before he succumbed to cancer and released his last shallow breath. Jim had flown out a couple of days earlier, after we had got a phone call that his dad was nearing the end.

My dad, at the time, was in a nursing home in Vancouver, living with Alzheimer's. He would forget that he was supposed to call the nurse for help getting out of bed and kept injuring himself, falling on an elbow repeatedly when he needed to pee in the middle of the night. So while Jim flew to Houston, I stayed home to spend a few more days with my father. Jim's stepdad would die on the following Tuesday.

I got the call about *my* dad on that Sunday morning. It was his doctor.

"I'm sorry to tell you this, but your dad passed away this morning." Then a few explanations. "You can come out to see him before they take him off the ward."

Plans changed. No flight to Houston. Drive out to the hospital. It was such an odd juxtaposition. One father a couple of days away from death and my own father today. They had never met each other and yet there was a connection.

As I raced around getting dressed and gulping down a coffee, a song flitted through my head — "And the Angels Sing."

Benny Goodman. Dad's favorite musician. My dad was there in my kitchen!

His soul was not in the body that I viewed in the hospital. The nurses had already cleared out all the extraneous hospital equipment from his room. His body lay under a white sheet, his face still as wax. I marveled at how a lifetime of loving and thinking, decisions and actions, had created this physical presence stretched out in front of me. But he was not there. His face was sunken. His profile reminded me of photographs I had viewed of so-called defective people on whom the Nazis had done horrific experiments. That is not how I knew my dad. The flesh and blood had fallen away so that the hawk nose and receding chin bore no resemblance to the face of the handsome man my dad had been.

But his younger self came back to my kitchen to listen to the Benny Goodman music I played that evening. I filled the kitchen with the love song my dad had sent me. Was it about my mother, dancing with her in his arms in their early years? I have no way of knowing. Regardless, I was sure it was for me to hear. We had a wonderful farewell as we shared the music and I spent all my tears.

Recently I found a meditation I had written on the evening of his death, which was not so coincidentally also the birthday of his mother. Apparently I had visualized this next to my dad's deathbed.

"Standing next to my dad's deathbed, I saw an image of a warrior, like a Roman warrior soldier," I had written. As I did, my higher guidance kicked in and gave me deeper insight into my father's remarkable life — remarkable as I saw it.

My guides intoned: "He was a warrior in many lifetimes. A soldier of means, always. And filled with pleasure, looking after his family — a pleasure for him in this lifetime, and the transformation away from the need to fight was a rest — a well-deserved rest for his soul, a completion enveloped in a loving family."

He had really been the one of my two parents who instilled in me a sense of power and possibility. He was a wonderful role model for a life of success and the ability to be happy.

The Friday after Dad's memorial, I felt finished. I wrote that I was satisfied that I gave a good eulogy. I gave it from my heart, and I also felt "I don't want to let him go yet. I will never let him go in my memory." Despite his disciplinarian approach during my younger years, my father taught me to be independent, to do things and to take on challenges, to make amends to no one, and to let it be. The stifling of my spiritual understanding remained regardless of all that I learned from having him as a dad, but I was to later learn that this was a result of many lifetimes.

I reflected that my dad had the patience of Job with my mother's nagging — what a wonderful man. At this point in my meditations, I heard my father's voice come through: "She was a headache, wasn't she? But you know we were all happy in a big family, and I had such a wonderful work life, such a challenging, stimulating work life that the barbs that came from your mom were more like a little dog nipping at the heels. She was very successful as my partner and supporter. She was wonderful in helping me with my communication while entertaining in the world. She supported the flamboyant self within me. She could have been more if she wasn't so shy, but she was beautiful and did love to be escorted out, so we made a good team."

About a month later, another message came through: "I enjoyed your wedding, and I was very happy to see you happy with Jim. Jim is always hesitant and needs to be prodded. You know this. Now where you and Jim are concerned, he needs to sand off some rough edges. Love your life and live your life. Do what you want to do. Don't think about what I did. Do what you want to do. You're a good little investor. You are a beautiful woman.

"We're driving together my daughter … we're driving together.

I will pop in every once in a while. I'm not here to judge you or tell you what to do. I am here to support you. You need to shine like I did — OK?"

My dad has popped back in several times, one time telling me that he was around my youngest niece. When I told her this, I thought she would balk at the idea, but she said, "No. I do believe it. He always told me I was his favorite."

My dad dropped in again more recently, during a reading I had with a medium, Ara Parisien. She told me, "Your dad says that he didn't understand you when he was alive, but he understands you now."

"Well," I said, "that is a wonderful message because I know my dad was disappointed that I didn't follow a scientific path in my life." He had delighted in teaching me algebra before we learned it in school, and I had excelled at both math and art, but I ultimately followed a more artistic, creative path. This was what I needed to continue to do to delve deeper into my inner self. But first I had to learn to trust my intuition that had drawn me into the spiritual realm.

I vowed to use the memory of my father's successful life to guide mine. Done.

SOUL FAMILIES

I am familiar with the idea that we each choose our family before being born. So, it is not difficult now to understand that the issues I had with my parents were challenges for me to learn and grow from. I understand why my mother was so judgmental, why I felt emotionally abandoned even in her physical presence. I understand why I had such a wonderful relationship with my father.

But while writing this book, new, deeper insights about my

connections to family members have been revealed to me. By healing aspects of myself, I am healing a line of people from whom they were passed down.

FAMILY CHILDREN

As I meditated one day, I received a message about new family members. This became the beginning of a discussion on new generations and what they are here to do personally and as a group for the world's healing. It was just a taste of knowledge to come ......

"Changelings will be born soon into your family — three within your family. Two will live within reach. The third will be across the pond. She will have her child before she knows it."

The guides were obviously working to bring new energy to my family. They told me: "We will contribute to the development of the young ones. We will provide the spiritual flow that will buoy up their ambitions and their fluid minds. Turn up the heat on your own ambitions."

I interpreted this as a reminder to be aware that I have an important role to play with the young ones entering the earth plane.

SOUL NEEDS AND FAMILY CONSCIOUSNESS

More from guides: "Now, if we look at the bigger picture, we will see that all manner of exploration in the world is driven by the soul's choice and need for experience of a particular kind for its own development. The choice is the soul's prerogative with discussion through its spiritual connections before entering the earth plane. Each family of souls, as you are beginning to learn, have a particular bent. Now, you may use the families of consciousness as a guideline as outlined in Jane Roberts's books by her spirit guide Seth.

"There are other systems of categorization abounding in the universe, but you have correctly associated yourself to what is called the Sumari, the creative family outlined in the Seth books, whose purpose is to provide the cultural, spiritual, and artistic heritage for humanity. You are particularly interested in the Gramada family — 'organizers, founders of large businesses, statesmen, politicians, vital, active, creatively aggressive since they are endowed with the creativity of the mind.'[1] This is why you are so fascinated by the politics of the United States. The US has been on the precipice of outlining to the world a new creative mode of being that will become apparent in the years following the election (between Trump and Biden). As the many who are projecting their minds into spirit are sourcing information from the spirit arena, powerful new ideas and waves of philosophy will flood into the world. There will be a shift. You have leapt across the chasm with this election."

From what I see in the news, I don't perceive this happening, but maybe we are meant to have faith that it is in the works, underneath the surface.

Do we need to look deeper — or higher?

A POLITICAL FOOTBALL

I've tried to tone down the political rhetoric in this book while still getting across a message that needs discussing on the topic of families.

Because abortion seems to be part of every election in the US, perhaps it is time to look at the topic from a different perspective —

---

1 Roberts, Jane. *The Unknown Reality* Vol. 2, Session 736. Amber-Allen Publishing, Inc., 1997 (or. 1979).

one that goes beyond our earthly understanding and relates directly to a discussion on family.

My guides told me that this is an important topic at this point in history: "As we see it now, in earthly terms, it is a visceral argument that has nothing to do with the high-minded exploration of inner personal power. It puts the power in the hands of politicians and religious leaders whose main interest is in their own power to control the masses for their own benefit. Politicians pull this topic out of a hat because it is so emotionally charged — they falsely label it 'killing babies.'

"Here, we discuss the idea of abortion in terms of the soul's need for expression in the physical world. The soul, who has decided upon a particular woman to be born to for its own purposeful development, does not necessarily attach to the fetus, and therefore can enter and exit the physical realm up until the birthing process begins. Now, when this occurs, the soul will step into the body of the baby as it is born. Up until this point, the soul has free discretion as to how much experience it wishes to have within the fetus.

"The soul that may have been attached to a fetus that aborts itself may be relieved. Choice is always there for the soul in conjunction with the woman on a spirit level in dreams. When a fetus is aborted, the soul that has claimed it may need to find another avenue to enter physical life. The soul may maintain its intention to be part of its original family choice or it may decide that there are other options for it to incarnate within the psychological and physical realm of another person or family circumstance. There is much more fluidity of the soul once it has entered the Spirit realm to decide when and where and with whom to come back into physical body based on its own purposeful goals."

I will add that, based on the flexibility of the soul, the intended mother has complete choice as to whether a child will enhance her personal and spiritual development or not. The reasons for the choice may be conscious or unconscious, but it is her decision and responsibility to be made or claimed as she chooses, unfettered by societal norms.

Invitation to Reflect

To accept that you chose your family is the ultimate in taking personal responsibility. It is a good place to start when thinking about your life's purpose. You gave yourself a starting place for your life. With this clarity, it should give you clues how to move forward. It should also help you see how to take full responsibility for your future and therefore be more self-directed and intentional in your actions. I was fortunate to gain more understanding about my choice from Jonas.

Q. With this understanding that you chose the people in your life before entering physicality, ask yourself: Who most supported me in my life force, in the development of my character? Who helped me become who I am today? Who loved me the most? Do I see why it is these *particular* people?

Can you thank them, in your mind, for all they did for you?

4

FAT BE GONE

Life is a banquet, and most poor suckers are starving to death.
— Rosalind Russell in *Auntie Mame*

In the dim light I sit, a small skinny boy on a wooden bench at a table rustic and scarred by years of use. The room, heated by a wood stove, is small and dank. A large woman in a grubby apron is yelling abusive words at me. "Shut up, you! No, you cannot have more stew!" Fear and rage well up in my throat. I can no longer tolerate the abuse from my mother, and I bolt out the door to wander the cobblestone streets alone.

I am so hungry that I take a loaf of bread from a street vendor's table. Whistles blow and a watchman grabs me. I am thrown into a dark prison as a boy of twelve, left to starve to death within its stone walls.

"Oh wow." I pop out of my vision. "So that's why I have never wanted to fast."

I immediately recognized the woman in this vision as my mother in this life. I still remember where I was as this vision materialized. I was walking towards my grandmother's home to take her dog out for a walk, and I must have begun daydreaming.

This vision of a lifetime in the Middle Ages came to me as I began a weight-loss diet and boosted my determination to drop the excess fat I was carrying around which was not serving my health or a vibrant life. Lesson learned: I don't need to hold on to the anxiety that there will not be enough food in case I need it in the future. I have plenty of food to nourish me in my life now.

Because I love fashion and clothing, being overweight was an issue. I had a hard time finding styles I liked in beautiful fabrics. So I resorted to "girly" things that I had previously eschewed in the past. "I can still buy shoes that I love," I reasoned, and there began my collection. Nails and makeup took me further into girly-land and I have never left since, but more on that later ......

MOTHER

My mother showed her love for me through clothes. She would parade the two of us through the golf club dining room in matching dresses she had proudly sewn herself. Yes, I belonged to her!

On the surface, my mom and I had a good relationship that belied the undercurrent of fear I felt of being criticized and judged by her. Yet another reason to be a good girl. Looking back, I realize she had been my guide in all matters image — how to behave, how to dress, how to appeal to people. She created beautiful gardens admired by neighbors, spent hours dividing and transplanting Shasta daisies and other glorious, vibrant flowers in the front garden. She painted our homes in trendy color schemes. Our living room became avocado green when avocado green was the look. She sewed amazing clothes, first for my dolls and later for me. When I was a child, she dressed me in hand-smocked dresses with little puff sleeves made by my grandmother into the years when they were too short, then in dresses she made that were too long in the Twiggy era — the advent of the miniskirt.

My mom kept me up to date with the trends, even if the hems were too long. Other girls in school would roll up the waistbands of their kilts, turning our school uniforms into sexy little bits of tartan barely covering their butts. I was too shy and so lived in mine as it was made to be, with pleats swaying nicely and politely behind.

One particular outfit stands out in my mind. Mom always made me clothes for Christmas. The year when I was fourteen, I opened the squishy package and pulled out an iridescent peach Naugahyde — read thick faux leather used for upholstery — skirt and jacket. The seams had uncut threads and the intended buttons were still on the cardboard card. Everything about it screamed *too much* for me as a shy five-foot-ten teenager who towered above everyone else at school. I'm certain the dismay that showed clearly on my face hurt my mom's feelings deeply. The unfinished suit lay on the sewing table for weeks until one day it disappeared — I guess mom had given up on the idea of making me into the runway model she saw in her mind. I was finally relieved of my guilt of not satisfying her dreams. While I did learn style from her, I carried the feeling of not being enough for my mother throughout my adult life.

It took my father's memorial to break me of that ingrained habit of thought.

RELEASE

"I wish she would die!" The words spat out of my mouth to my husband as we drove home from the memorial service. "I hate her!"

The eulogy I had just given was the culprit. As I stood in front of the altar and poured out my heart about the father I had loved so much, my mom was twitching and twiddling her fingers together in distress. I knew what it was about. She thought I was going too long. I told of the period he was a navigator in the Air Force, a man of his time, using the stars Castor and Pollux to guide the blacked-out plane to its German targets. Half the audience there was quietly staring at me, sitting in their military uniforms. I teared up when someone played "Taps" and the bagpipe led us out into the sunshine.

On that fateful drive home, when I allowed myself to express my true feelings, Jim turned his head towards me and told me Mom had been repeating, "Too long. Too long," and he had tapped gently on her shoulder and said, "Jean, relax. She's doing fine."

"How could she *do* that to me?! How could she worry about what other people would think of her more than what I was sharing about my dad?" I needed to calm down — I had the steering wheel in my hands.

A few days later, I replayed the story for my counselor. She asked if my mom had a group of friends to support her.

"Yes," I said. "She has a group of widows who meet every day at McDonald's for coffee."

"Well then," she said, "you no longer need to be your mother's representative in the world"— my mom's expression of my role in the family and for keeping her good image intact.

It was a sea shift, a mind shift, a clearing of guilt. My body relaxed. I was free to be me. No hesitation. No inner criticism. No self-doubt.

I was free to be myself. After all the therapy groups, personal growth seminars, and spiritual journeys, this one counselor had said the magic words.

CONFIRMATION

It was not long after the eulogy that I consciously chose to use my dad as a role model. He had a zest for life, was happy as a successful business man. Better to model myself after him than the anxiety-driven, emotional yet controlling woman that my mother modelled.

In a session, I once told my therapist that I was confused because my mother was there but I felt like I had been abandoned. She said that I was correct, that she was not there emotionally. I recently read an article in the *New York Times* about a book written by a woman who experienced something similar. The dedication expresses it clearly: "To the motherless child who somehow survived all that was missing even when Mother was there." The book is Jasmin Lee Cori's *The Emotionally Absent Mother*. It appears this is becoming a popular topic of conversation.

After much soul-searching and a lot of time, I realized my mom had shared her special gift with me and my family. I now credit my mother with being the glue that brought so many members of both sides of my family together into a vibrant and elevating collective of people. She brought her mother, Nannan, into our home and into my life when I was thirteen, a time when I most needed the love that my grandmother could give me.

I received an interesting message from Jonas that reiterates what I have written about my mother ... surprisingly in a few of the same words: "Your mother came into the world to be the glue to keep people in the family together. When she passed, she was magnificently cradled by the gems of her own life's purpose — the family that held her dear to their hearts, her sister and brothers. They gave her love, and she gives it back. She now understands your situation, but her work with you was done. She will return for her own sake to enjoy a life of pleasant activities and love given to her by her new chosen family."

It was important to see my mother as an individual, and the message from Jonas helped me understand her as a woman with a soul path that was not exclusively one of being a mother. Perhaps she transmitted that independent spirit to me. When she passed, I was told by my guides that she was reviewing her life with her sister. I imagine that she knows I have great support from others in the family, alive and in spirit.

FOOD FOR THOUGHT

I began this chapter with the story about food and my mother in a medieval lifetime. Food is associated with mothers in a deep way. Whatever issue we have with food can be connected to our relationships with our mothers. I am not alone in struggling with weight. It is emotional, of course. But as an adult, it's up to me to take care of myself. I offer some thoughts. One day as I ate my salad lunch, I wrote this poem:

There is a world in my bowl
Salt from the Himalayas
Pepper from Vietnam
Cabbage and carrots from Salinas
Balsamic vinegar and olive oil from Italy

A tomato from my friend Sylvia's garden
Bowl made of porcelain clay from China
White glaze created with sand that covers the Earth's
beaches
All in a 6" x 4" space.

Mindfulness, appreciation of the fecundity of the world, brings us into alignment with our Earth.

My guides explained this in another way: "Each one of you holds every part of this world within your body. With the food you eat — all forms of food — all parts of the world bring this together: the vanilla from Madagascar, the spices from India, maybe herbs from your windowsill, tea from Asia, coffee from many countries of the world, the biologics from the Amazon. This is about incorporating all the places of the world into your bodies, through your breath, through your food, through your water. Particles of the whole Earth are unifying in combination with all peoples."

In light of this, can we really dishonor other people and places?

More from the guides: "The political backlash against other countries that you feel today has much to do with the fear of the unknown, the unknown person. But the fear of the unknown person reflects a deeper fear within each person of the changes that are developing. There is an understanding on a cellular level that you are on the brink of a change — the Age of Aquarius — which cannot be turned back. The change is inevitable. The weakest links are the ones who fear the change the greatest. The old values of power over people are receding. You are beginning to more deeply understand that there is value in everyone and in everyone's contribution. This is feeding movements such as Black Lives Matter and the Empowerment of Women which have been picked up all over the world. These things are propelling you into a future of great beauty and creativity."

The beautiful salad was part of my last weight-loss diet — my guides weighed in with their own thoughts: "As you say, you are not alone. Your body will be healed through movement, food, the power of your mind, and the power of breath. Consider your time with a diet as the final cleansing of the palate, and the body's strength will be returned. You can no longer face the world with fear of eating the wrong thing. So do not speak any longer about your inability to cut out sugars, about your inability to *not* gain weight. Do not speak these thoughts. You are just telling your body to perpetuate these problems. There is no need to fear food! Taste your food and put your fork down when you know you've had enough."

"Easier said than done," I thought.

The day I completed the diet, this is what came to me: "What I eat will be used in the most positive manner within my body. All that is not of assistance to my body will be left and eliminated. My body will love what I give it and will use it to create a beautiful strength which I inhabit as a soul with purpose."

Perhaps I have somewhat cleared the issue of body image that plagued me and my mother. All I know is that the young women in my family are more conscientiously aware of being healthy and keeping fit than when I was young. Maybe I was part of a guinea pig generation!

DNA and Soul's Purpose

Here is a message from the guides about physicality: "The structure of your body is supported by the food you eat, and it is also supported by the thoughts you think. Your DNA, the blueprint of your body, is affected by both. You talk to your body, you talk to your DNA. DNA is a chemical construction that can be active or passive depending on what is focused upon in the mind. The mind bends the purpose of the DNA to the purpose of the soul. As the soul asserts itself, the DNA that supports the journey is activated and problematic DNA that is not supportive of the soul's purpose can be deactivated by repeating positive affirmations.

"For instance, every person has stronger issues and weaker issues within the physical being. Now, the body is well versed in using the strong, powerful organs to compensate for the not-so-powerful organs. Structure within the body is protein, fat, salt, and water. You metabolize your food to support your physical being. There are a multitude of options for the body to work with to create optimum performance. So, as you consider your options regarding diet, supplements, and exercise routines, those that resonate with you are those that are optimally going to support your body structure in terms of the mix that is required within your system. Therefore, as you choose those things that resonate with you, you are optimizing your body's peak performance as it stands at the moment. So, one particular chemical response in your body may be obviously fantastic in your system and it does nothing for someone else. To put it more simply, 'one person's elixir is another person's poison.' There are no rules. Trust your own body."

INVITATION TO PLAY OR WRITE

In a meditation, I was told to have some fun with my family by imagining each person as a bird, which in nature represents spirit. What bird suits the personality of each one? This sent me to the internet to find pictures of birds. I settled on a pink cockatoo for myself, like the ones I saw in Australia, and a black cockatoo for my guy.

I won't share what I envisioned for the rest of my family, but it was a fun way to see each person in a more objective light and remove some emotional baggage I was carrying around about family relations.

This game is a good way to rise above our childhood issues and gain clues into why we behave the way we do in certain situations.

Q. What bird would you be?

OR

You may need to delve deeper and work through emotional issues. Journaling can be a useful way to uncover thoughts you are unaware of, especially if you do it as automatic writing. This works best if you set a timer for seven minutes, start with a statement prompt, and then write nonstop whatever comes into your mind.

Writing Prompt

My relationship with my mother (or another person) was ...

My relationship with food/diet culture/my body is ...

My path to healing looks like ...

My path to strength looks like ...

5

CALIFORNIA, COMING HOME

Nothing is left to chance. The choreography of players
and circumstances is plotted with mind-numbing precision.
Enormous forces of attraction are activated and engaged.
The odds for your inevitable success begin skyrocketing.
And every second of every day is calibrated and recalibrated ...
for every thought you think.

— **Mike Dooley,** *Notes from the Universe*

PURPOSE AND LIGHT

"Well," I said to Jim, "I guess we've settled enough for me to relax and begin my morning meditations again."

I was sitting in lotus position, or as close to lotus style as my legs would allow, on the slice of foam purchased as a mattress for our three-month sojourn in California. An unfurnished apartment in a courtyard-style building with a central swimming pool became our temporary home. Naturally for such a short stay, we had wanted a furnished place, but it was the time before Airbnb and nothing with a stick of furniture was available. This apartment was vacant only because the manager had been unable to rent it out. Sawdust speckled the living room's shaggy brown carpet — he had been using it as a workshop. We offered him three months' rent up front and moved in.

The bedroom had weird vibes, not only because the room had only one piece of furniture. I had to get to the bottom of this. I put my hand on the wall. Chills ran through my body … I knew someone had been murdered there … A lover's fight, or a gay lover's fight, was the answer, which I later told to a neighbor. She looked at me in disbelief.

"How do you know that?" she asked.

"Well … I'm psychic," I explained. "I am sensitive to energy and can detect energy in a room." I had just used psychometry as I had learned in Victoria. She was quite intrigued, but I was still hesitant to say too much to people I didn't know.

My job while we were there was to continue to get the feel of life in the LA sunshine — not an onerous task. Jim's job was the same, but he was also reconnecting with old friends and colleagues, trying to decide if he could again fit in with the zeitgeist of the city sixteen years after leaving it. It was there that he had done the big switch from living on an aircraft carrier in the US Navy in the South Pacific to being a beach bum, surfing the waves in the glorious California sun, before eventually buckling down to an education in art and design. In California, Jim's sculpture, a combination of conceptual and constructed pieces, had been in vogue when he lived there.

We spent many Saturdays wandering through the collection of galleries, referred to as the "Art Mall" of Santa Monica, at famous artists' openings. It was often difficult to maintain a sense of decorum around the movie stars we saw. No one asks for autographs in places like these!

So here we were, loving the sun and the energetic craziness of Venice Beach, following our hearts — to what? Maybe a new life adventure of living here permanently?

Turning my mind inward, as Jim tapped out his CV on his borrowed typewriter, I tried to find a way back into the peace of mindfulness that allowed for spiritual travel. The links were still there, and I climbed my mind ladder to join forces with Jonas. There, as I sat, Jonas unfolded the reason for my life. My focus was to understand the gradual progression of the individual to self-actualization through the history of humankind — big picture stuff. Out of the darkness into the light. Whoa!

Mass consciousness, as it developed in pre–World War II Europe, to individual consciousness, personal power. We were moving into the Aquarian Age. The march of time brought periods of great carnage designed by one master orchestrator before periods of great breakthroughs, insights, and revolutions to reset the power structures.

"You have lived through and witnessed the progressions and digressions throughout history." I knew that Jonas was speaking on a grand scale, referring to the past life memories I had been experiencing. At the same time, in my current lifetime, America and the world were going through massive shifts in consciousness with anti-war protests, the Civil Rights movement, a new wave of female power, the increase in activism for gay rights during and after the AIDS crisis …… He concluded by saying, "It's time to be a revealer of the truth — to thine own self be true — become the rising star of your own life."

This was a call to me to open up. It felt daunting. But I did take to heart his statement "You will begin this new trajectory by offering classes like Kitty's in psychic development and meditation."

As I continued my daily meditations, a new past life filtered into my mind. Interestingly, while living in Venice Beach, California, I saw myself standing in a square in Venice, Italy, with Jim and another artist friend of ours, all of us in long robes. I deduced we were philosophers and/or teachers. I instantly knew that Venice was the crossroads of East and West, that it had been not only the trading place for spices, silks, and money, but the magical place where philosophies from Asia permeated Europe. It was the most exciting place to be in the early Renaissance.

Many years later, on my trip to attend the Venice Biennale, the preeminent global art exhibition, I received confirmation of my links there. On a hazy day, I stepped off the vaporetto, the waterbus, onto the cobblestone pavers of the Piazza San Marco, past a column topped by the lion of the city. As I walked into the square, my feet sent flocks of pigeons into the air and tears ran down my cheeks. The sentence "I haven't been here for a very long time" ran through my mind. I was coming home to another lifetime, and this Venetian lifetime seemed to personify the forward progression of humanity, one more building block in my understanding.

The connection between the Venice Beach of Los Angeles and Venice, Italy, seems obvious to me now. They were/are cities of great change and optimism.

* * *

I thrived in Los Angeles, joining a spiritual group, dipping my hands in clay at a pottery class, viewing world-class art, and spying movie stars going about their daily lives. What a thrilling place! I loved my morning swims in the courtyard pool — it all gave me an aliveness that I didn't feel in Victoria. I wanted to be there. But Jim could not get back in the groove. He seemed unnerved by the successes his friends had achieved while he was teaching in a small city on isolated Vancouver Island. So we decided we would head back to Victoria, not victorious.

Goodbye, Hello

My last evening at Spirit Class in Los Angeles was a memorable one. I said my goodbyes to all and left the building. Walking down the sidewalk, a voice called out from behind me.

"Are you the woman who sees souls?" She caught my attention.

I turned to a woman I hadn't seen in class before. Thinking for a moment, I replied, "Yes."

"I haven't attended these evenings for a while, but I felt compelled to come tonight. I knew I needed to tell someone about a dream I had last night," she explained. "In the dream, I was on a bus and I met a person who could see people's souls."

And there she was, asking if that was me. She went on to tell me a story she had heard about a group of women prisoners in Auschwitz who had lice. Rather than being a horrible thing, the lice had repulsed the Nazi guards and kept these women safe from being raped. In adversity can be salvation. Next, she told me I needed to continue my psychic work. "You need to teach others to open their minds."

"Well, that was interesting," I thought as I walked away, amazed at the connections the mind can make and mesmerized by how my guides sent me instructions through a stranger. (I did start teaching upon returning to Victoria — I started my first meditation group.)

After the conversation, I pondered her mention of Nazi Germany — it was intriguing. The lifestyle I was enveloped in, in the wonderland of Los Angeles, couldn't have been further from life under the authoritarian regime of Nazi Germany.

Just before heading out for this summer sojourn, I had been "treated" to some anxiety-provoking scenes from what I came to know as my last lifetime. I had learned during Kitty's classes that my last lifetime had been in Nazi Germany, that I had been a soldier. In a meditation in class, I had glimpses of that lifetime as an Austrian soldier, waltzing in Vienna with a beautiful woman whom I later became engaged to. I twirled her around a dance floor at a ceremonial military ball.

The awareness of being in the war in Germany also came to me during the American presidential campaign as George H. W. Bush — the first one — was running for president. I had connected to some reporting — true or not — that Bush was somehow linked to the Nazis, and I was in a panic about him becoming president.

In psychic class, I opened my eyes after a meditation to see three other people in the circle staring at me like I was on trial. My inner mind told me this was about my actions in Germany in my last lifetime. My fear about Bush Sr. becoming president had been a clue for my past life exploration.

My mother told me that when I was a baby I would not be held, that I'd push my little body away with outstretched arms, my hands against any chest that tried to snuggle me. Maybe something had occurred in that last lifetime that had caused such behavior? Or perhaps it had to do with jumping back into the world without much time passing in between lives. I can only speculate.

More about my lifetime in Germany came crashing in on me

many years later, in another chapter of my life ......

For now, it was time for me and Jim to go back home and expand on our ever-growing need for life and new experiences.

THE RIGHT PLACE?

Arriving back in the sleepy burgh of Victoria didn't sit right with me. I was not interested in being back in a city that seemed suspended in the year 1911 — the vintage of our house. Time to fly the coup again.

But how the hell was I going to get Jim on board? He seemed to want to retreat to the hills of Sooke, a sleepy village even further west of Civilization where he could lick the wounds of his damaged ego. The aggressiveness of the art scene in Los Angeles had left him feeling forgotten, and he was not interested in moving to a big city. But for me, Vancouver held the promise of expanding my life experience.

Knowing I wanted to move off the Island, we decided to explore locations we wouldn't see again. One Saturday we headed west up the coast, past the log-strewn beaches accessed through mystic ancient forests of cedar and ferns, to a little tea house and cabin getaway called Point No Point. We sat at the simple table sipping English tea and munching scones and cakes, homemade by the owners. It was a lovely afternoon spent gazing out the plate glass windows onto the powerful endless waves of the Pacific Ocean. But the peace was shattered as we exited the tranquility of the dining room and Jim announced, "I don't want to move to Vancouver. I want to live out here."

Stunned, I replied, "I will divorce you if you don't want to go with me." I was serious. My insides had turned upside down. I was not ready to retire and die.

So, as I had envisioned, within a year we had sold our house. The entire moving enterprise had taken some major finagling on my part, with the undeniable help of my guides. How to get over Jim's obstinate nature was the question. Finding him a teaching job was the answer.

I sat to meditate on the question: "Is there anywhere in Vancouver that has a job opening?" The answer came immediately — Langara College. Right away I called the school and was put through to the secretary of the fine art department.

"There will be a job posting for a full-time position for a year to take over for an instructor who is going on sabbatical."

"Where will I be able to find out about it?"

"It will be posted in the newspaper."

"Thanks. I'll keep my eye open for it," I said and hung up.

I called my mom to ask her to occasionally scan the want ads in the Vancouver paper for the position, and then I forgot about it.

Somehow, I managed to convince Jim that the move would be a good thing, and we set about fixing all the little unfinished details in the house and put it on the market. My mom and dad took the ferry over to Victoria for the day to view the house as it was set up for the open. This was long before either of my parents had passed away. They were happy with my marriage to Jim and supportive of the projects we did together — the renovation of our Victorian-style house being one of them. We had spent a lot of time and effort on giving the place the appearance of an art gallery, with crisp white walls and original artwork. It looked beautiful to everyone. Even our realtors were impressed.

After everyone left the open house, I remembered about asking Mom to check the job postings and called her about it again. She called back to say there was a posting for Langara College in the paper. Jim sent in his resume.

The next day, Jim headed to Vancouver for an interview at Langara College. A week later, Jim was offered the job and the house deal went through. Whew!

We received three offers for our house after two days on the market. There was one from a young couple who wrote a lovely letter saying they really wanted to live there, a full price offer from an investor, and one other. I was torn. I really wanted to give the house to the couple who, like Jim and I had been, were just getting started. Tuning inward, my guides gave me assistance in choosing which offer to accept. They recommended we accept the full price offer from the investor, which was best for our financial future in Vancouver. My heart went out to the others, but a couple of years later we discovered that the investor had to spend a lot of money to install a completely new drainage system around the house. He was able to afford this, but I imagine the young couple would not have. The perspective from the higher level viewed by my guides proved we had made the right decision. We didn't know the entire reason for the advice, but we had followed it anyway.

To say I had some help from the other side is an understatement.

Next, we needed to find our new home. One morning in our rented house after the move to Vancouver, I picked up the newspaper from the front door and asked Jonas in frustration, "Where is our house?" I had already spent several months scouring neighborhoods in search of a home that suited both us and our bank account. I was directed to the ads in the newspaper.

I noticed a listing for a place in a suburb of Vancouver. "Oh, I don't want to live that far from the city center." But Jonas had directed me to the only modern-style house on the market, and so off we drove to see this place. Arriving early at the house that backed onto a creek in a wooded ravine, I suggested we drive around.

"Turn left, go down this back alley" — Jim, for once, followed my instructions as we drove. We found ourselves in front of a house we had seen earlier in the fall. It had not been up for sale at that time, but we had sat in the cul-de-sac, admiring it. "Wouldn't it be amazing if we could buy a house like that," we had said to each other, never imagining we could afford it. This time there was a for sale sign. Change of plans. Quickly we viewed the original house we had driven there to see. The realtor happened be the same one on the listing up the hill.

"We want to see *that* house."

It was spectacular. Half of the house was cantilevered over a carport, jutting out towards a treed ravine. The living space was on the second level — it had wrap-around floor-to-ceiling windows with a view of Mount Baker in Washington State in the distance to the southeast. Windows from the dining area and kitchen looked south and west to a leafy ravine. The location, set far back from the street, pleased Jim, who would have lived in a forest wilderness if I'd let him. He joked about building ramparts with machine gun turrets at the end of the driveway. Go figure!

I loved it. It suited me perfectly. With birdsong sparkling in the air, it seemed like an oasis from the city noise and traffic. From the minute we stepped into the house, it felt like it was ours. Standing in the 1970s kitchen, which I definitely would be renovating, I called our mortgage broker. With two additional rental suites in the house to create a large income, it was perfect. Our mortgage was approved on the spot. I was extremely grateful to Jonas for all his guidance. Jim had been oblivious to all the spiritual dealing I had done, but it proved to me that if you ask, it shall be given. Seek and ye shall find. You only need to ask and then take action when your intuition says "go." It was where we both were meant to be.

As my guides had urged me while in California, I began a new psychic/meditation group. Within another year I had transferred all my design skills from graphics to designing and executing corporate events in downtown luxury hotels. Every bit of life had fallen into place as I tuned in with my daily meditations — every bit, including the ultimate job for Jim; every bit, as I conjured our most perfect designer house on the edge of a forested ravine that we transformed into a hotbed of creativity and love.

Life was exciting.

Still, downtown Vancouver beckoned me. The city was filled with high-rise towers that reignited my love of modern design. My fascination with glass and steel condo towers began there.

On a day when the sun was hovering low on the western horizon, I was driving east on 49th Avenue, going over a rise in the road, when I was treated to a glimpse of the towers of New Westminster in the distance, glistening with windows gilded by the setting sun. It seemed like a picture from the fairy tales my dad used to read to me. Something timeless and magical was held in that vision.

As time passed, I continued to lead a meditation group and I moved on from designing events to redesigning homes. So began the renovation and real estate phase of my life. Jim followed along after he retired from teaching.

I still wanted to live in one of those magical towers, but it was not yet time.

INVITATION TO MEDITATE

Meditation has become the way I sort out many of the questions and problems in my life. So many of the successes I wrote about in this chapter were facilitated by meditation. If I feel out of sorts in the morning, I realize it's because I haven't meditated. Meditation grounds me, and I usually come out of it with a clear picture of how to proceed with my day.

So, if you don't already meditate regularly, then it's time you begin. I know, there are lots of excuses. "I don't have time" is number one. I say, if you don't have at least ten minutes to give to yourself to sit quietly and clear your mind, then you don't have quality time and attention to give to others.

Some people say that being in nature is their meditation. Great. Others, running or yoga. Many forms of meditation involve the breath, slowing it down and focusing on it. There are many free lessons on the internet that can teach you how to meditate. I have discovered that humming or chanting OHM through an octave and corresponding chakras of my body is the best way for me to open my mind to higher vision.

Q. What is the easiest method for you to quiet your mind and rise to a higher level of vibration?

Each of the seven major chakras — energy centers along

the axis of the body — vibrate at a different level. The lowest grounds your body. The highest, the third eye and crown chakras, involve intentionally tapping into the energy of the universe by letting go of your rational thoughts and allowing your mind to float upward.

6

DING-DONG, THE WITCH IS DEAD

Because in the end, you won't remember the times you spent in the office or mowing your lawn. Climb that goddamn mountain.
— Jack Kerouac

SURPRISE, SURPRISE

At seven years old, I had nightmares about the Wicked Witch from *The Wizard of Oz.*

The morning after participating in a psychic fair in the huge Vancouver Convention Centre, I climbed into a hot bath to soothe my fatigue.

I had spent the previous three days tuning in to innumerable people's energies to search for answers to their life dilemmas. This was my third year participating, and this year I had challenged myself to give a talk from the speaker's stage. Nervous but determined to break through my anxiety, I really put myself out there, albeit to an audience who had paid and wanted to be there. I don't remember what I spoke about, but I was proud of myself for doing it. After I left the stage, a woman from the audience came to speak with me. She said that the metal-rimmed glasses I was wearing were swirling a lot of distracting energy around my face and that I should at least consider plastic as a better choice. Her talent was obviously reading energy patterns that most people are oblivious to. I switched to contact lenses after that.

I met many interesting people doing the fairs. It gave me a lot of satisfaction to help others and perhaps impart some insights they could learn from. I even acquired a couple of new students for my meditation group after they visited my booth at a fair. They had been attracted to the booth, in part because of its backdrop — a six-foot-tall Egyptian screen I had painted with an image of Isis and Nefertari, the queen of Ramses II. One of these new students and I discovered that we had been soul sisters in Egypt. We also knew each other during the time when Jesus walked the Earth. We became very good friends, and both she and her husband went on to have successful careers in design fields in San Francisco and later in New York due to her ability to tune in to spirit.

Often during my psychic readings, I see visual images that the client will relate to despite my lack of understanding of their meaning. One person I read for that year, a psychic herself, told me that she and her family had just come back from Paris and were planning to start a business. Asking me what I saw, I told her I was seeing bicycles, not thinking this could be correct. To my surprise, she exclaimed that they had been thinking of going into the bicycle business. That was the encouragement she needed.

I had another client that year whom I was grateful to read for. I felt

I was tuning in to a beautiful soul. She was a high-powered woman who was working for a non-governmental organization in Africa. It is gratifying to assist such wonderful people.

Participating in the psychic fairs gave me confidence to continue doing readings, past life regressions, and guided meditation workshops on a small scale.

The morning after the fair, lying in the warm sudsy water of my bath, I tried to relax but instead fell into a dark fear. My body was permeated by an awareness that I had been a witch in a past life. I had been persecuted as a woman with great insights about how the world worked. Needing to shake free of this memory, I allowed my body to respond with muscular jerks until I finally calmed myself with the realization that I live in a safe world where it is OK to speak truth.

That lifetime was probably during the Inquisition in the early 1400s — when all of Europe was in the throes of Christian religious fervor and upheaval, perpetrating the atrocities of burning and torture of thousands for the crime of "devil worship." I will not go into the types of torture innocent women were subjected to, but I am sure everyone has heard of witch burning. Women with intuitive wisdom were persecuted then as they have been throughout history.

I was well aware that this vision came to me as a result of using my gifts that past weekend just as I had in my past lifetime. This was only the beginning of clearing some of the fear of being in my power that lingered in my psyche.

At the time of this revelation, I wasn't particularly interested in researching the monstrous acts perpetrated by the Christian church and political leaders for the purpose of enhancing their power. I still am not, although as I write, I quickly take a look at the Spanish Inquisition ... No, not going there — it turns my insides still.

I had a couple of friends in my meditation class I was connected to around this issue. One of my girlfriends was a witch in the same time frame but was not at all interested in talking about it. The same occurred with a young man in the group who told me he remembered being a priest in the Inquisition, and that was the end of that conversation. No one wants to see themselves doing evil acts, hurting others in another life.

Horrors

Sometimes I experience very difficult visions. I have had a vision of a man being pulled apart in the town square by horses stretching ropes that were tied to his hands and feet. I'm not sure if I was the tortured or the torturer, but I try to put such images out of my mind. I can't imagine what motivation can be behind such cruelty in the past and in the world today. When a male friend of mine told me he thought he had done bad things in a past life, this particular picture in the town square surfaced — not to be pursued! We are all witness to the abuses of power employed throughout history. We are being given the wherewithal in today's world to ensure these things are prevented from happening again. I'm not sure we are doing so well at that. But I know it is necessary to try.

Uncomfortable feelings from other lifetimes surfaced on trips to Europe with Jim. Snippets of lifetimes seeped in, leaving clues to stories I had already experienced or had yet to uncover. A trip to the Colosseum in Rome brought me great sadness — not for the Christians who had been mauled by lions but for the big cats who were abused, starved, and caged in dark caverns underneath the performance field of this ancient arena.

A tour through the Tower of London made me cringe. Jim gleefully passed from one display case to another, each containing spiked maces and all manner of weapons and torture devices. His choice while in the Navy to be a munitions officer on an aircraft carrier had a rich heritage in this torture chamber.

Not all locations in Europe held bad memories for me — thank God! Tripping along the winding country roads of Tuscany took us high into the many hill towns. Celebrations of the harvest and prosperity of the earth's bounty have been honored in these places over the centuries. This has given the region a benevolent energy that endures into the modern era. On a tour of the walled town of Monteriggioni, which offered many delightful Italian food shops, we entered through an ancient arched stone doorway into a shop where we were treated to a tasting of young, medium, and old pecorino. When I said "delicious!" the owner replied by turning the tip of her finger into her cheek — a simple sign meaning "fabulous, awesome, the best." Jim bought a round of the old cheese that he carried with him through to London and onto the plane to Vancouver. It was quite ripe upon arriving home.

Despite enjoying our bucolic tour, I was still aware of the energy of the hill towns of Tuscany being fortresses, places to retreat to and fight from to eliminate enemies who advanced on the surrounding lands. For most of its history, Italy was a country of warring states and kingdoms, only unifying as a country during the mid-to-late 1800s. The town of Monteriggioni was originally built in 1214 by the Republic of Sienna as a defensive fortification against the competing area of Florence. So, the relaxed atmosphere that most tourists experience while browsing the cheese and wine shops in this area was, for me, overlaid with the energy of its past.

A small town in Perugia, Spoleto, presented a totally different atmosphere. Seated for an evening meal with Jim at a café high on a hill overlooking the valleys of olive trees, their silver-leafed branches swaying in the breezes of time, I finally relaxed. The surrounding fields had been gifted by Julius Caesar to his successful generals as they returned from their campaigns to conquer the lands to the east of Rome. I resonated with this piece of history, with the rewards given for success in the ancient world, and was able to enjoy my glass of luscious red wine with a feeling of exhilaration. Italy held much past life history for me.

Germany is another story. I learned of the horrors perpetrated by the Nazis, and I was not interested in visiting Germany. At university, I had taken a course entitled "History of Revolutions" which featured a complete study of Hitler's Germany. This course sent me on a journey to understand how the people could be so manipulated by such an evil-minded man. I discovered it was either comply or die. Evidence was revealed to me over time that I was still carrying karma from that time period that was bleeding through into my current life. I discuss this in a later chapter as events in my life unfold.

INVITATION TO TRAVEL

Traveling is a wonderful way to open our minds, not only to new knowledge but to past life recall. I have experienced wonderful times and some not-so-wonderful times. Regardless, it has always expanded my understanding of myself.

Q. Have you ever experienced a sense of recognition of a place you were visiting for the first time? Were you drawn to research it more? What if you were to sit quietly and imagine yourself there? Try to allow a picture to open up that might reveal more to you.

7

ANOTHER MAN

I met a traveller from an antique land,
Who said—"Two vast and trunkless legs of stone
Stand in the desert. . . . Near them, on the sand,
Half sunk a shattered visage lies, whose frown,
And wrinkled lip, and sneer of cold command,
Tell that its sculptor well those passions read
Which yet survive, stamped on these lifeless things,
The hand that mocked them, and the heart that fed;
And on the pedestal, these words appear:
"My name is Ozymandias, King of Kings;
Look on my Works ye Mighty, and despair!"
Nothing beside remains. Round the decay
Of that colossal Wreck, boundless and bare
The lone and level sands stretch far away.

— Percy Bysshe Shelley, "Ozymandias"

A MAN OF POWER

I fell in love with Al Gore during the 2000 presidential election between him and George W. Bush. He was the one politician willing to talk about global warming and climate change. He had spent much of his time as Bill Clinton's vice president on the topic and wanted to continue to work on solutions. But that wasn't the first thing that drew me to him. My interest unfolded in a circuitous way as my guides gave me clues to follow.

On a trip to visit my friend Gail who had moved to Toronto, I was enjoying an evening of conversation in her living room after being introduced to her new friend Sue. At one point my mind opened up to a vision of the two women as politicians and friends in Babylon. I had previously seen myself in a lifetime with Gail as her wife when she was a male political figure in that ancient civilization. I had been interested in the hanging gardens and perhaps had been part of their creation. I mentioned my vision to them. Gail was a bit interested — she had been in my meditation group for many years and was familiar with my visions. But the conversation moved on quickly, and I sat in this enlightened state until the end of the evening when the name "Ozymandias" floated through my head.

After returning home to Vancouver, I sat to meditate one day and "Ozymandias, Ozymandias" kept running through my brain. I had to look it up. I found the poem of that name by Percy Shelley. Reading on, I discovered that the name "Ozymandias" was the Greek version of the name Ramses — Ramses II. Strange connections were materializing before my eyes. Being a daughter of this pharaoh, my interest was piqued.

Still on my search for answers, I researched a bit more and discovered that Al Gore had been nicknamed Ozymandias when he was in college. I was following the political career of the reincarnation of my father from ancient Egypt! I was sure he would be the next president. His loss devastated me.

A LIFE PURPOSE

After the election, I channeled a letter to Al Gore, with excerpts as follows:

"Your role in the world is far greater by not being president. You will be in a greater position of power to create good in the United States and for the whole Earth, mainly in the area of the environment. As vice president, you were involved in a branch of the government that will shift within the next ten years from being a small minority department to one of the larger departments. The idea is that if a government like that of the United States can spend billions of dollars on the manufacture of arms, in the training of men to battle in wars, why can't the country spend that money on battling another war — that of the degradation of our Earth. It is but a focus of will. It requires changing goals. It will require a whole new approach to life. Proactive rather than defensive. The military is all about defense — being able to guard, being able to protect. Direct this towards protecting the Earth rather than protecting us from other people and we would have a strong force for the betterment of the planet and the creation of many jobs for many people." I didn't have the nerve to send the letter to his website at the time.

At a later date, Jonas gave a character analysis and a reason why Al Gore's political loss was in line with his soul's purpose. It was also an example of how a loss may not truly be a loss but a redirection to put a soul back on a more purposeful path.

"Al Gore is a man with a great reputation for 'sticking to his guns' and for being determined to get a project completed. He's very well-known and will be unencumbered by the kind of strictures that the president is under. Now, it may feel like a failure to him to lose the presidency but he has a complete passion driving him to help the environment. This is really what his presidential campaign was about — to bring him into the forefront and to be respected by many Americans so that he can actually do the job he has divined for himself."

Recently I was struck by one of the 2016 Democratic candidates for president who said exactly what I had channeled then — that some of the funds that go to the military should be funneled into fighting climate change. Get the army to work on this. Beyond that, connect with other countries in the world to create an organization to do this.

Moving Forward

More information and predictions about politics come to me because I follow the politics of the US. What happens in the US affects the world in so many ways, especially in Canada. Political movements follow the development of humanity as we move through this space-time continuum.

"Now, fears of turning back the clock on powerful forward movements such as LGBTQ rights, abortion, health care for all, environmental concerns — these fears will not come to pass. They may not move forward as quickly as many wish, but the intention has been set to have them move forward and continue to progress into law. The population of the United States will not allow reversal or stagnation on these issues. You have seen how certain cities and states have moved forward despite federal attempts to shut down these issues, and they have been the proponents of movement forward."

I channeled this during the Trump administration, and already we are seeing some flaws in these arguments as I write. My hope is that I am viewing this from an all-too-small window of time. What was written next seems to indicate this:

"You all on Earth are moving forward on the wave of actualization of spirit living on Earth in purposeful manner. This is the new wave of the Aquarian Age which we have begun to speak about. Creative minds have tapped into the beginning of a movement that can start to heal, turning the mind away from animosities to build strength in numbers, strength as a whole rather than top down, to bring up the wisdom to all."

Power, Politics, and Atlantis

I continued to channel more insights during Trump's time in office ......

"Lewd behavior and obstructionism that is being performed at this time on the US political scene is of no avail against the powers that be in the realm of Spirit. You understand that there are families of spirit that are at play at the moment regarding politics and healing."

My understanding is that there is reciprocal interest from the powers in spirit and humans to work together to create positive results on the earth plane.

"The division between the Spirit realm and Earth is not as dense as you imagine. People's desire for change is heard by the Spirits who in turn send messages of guidance through dreams and intuition to those evolving people working in the political system and people in the general population who are purposefully raising their vibration for their own spiritual self-realization."

The law of attraction, easily translating to "like attracts like," is at play here. As people of high vibration connect, there will be a point at which the tides will turn and the Aquarian ideals of love, harmony, and understanding will dominate on the world stage and bring about change for good. In fact, I think we have gone over the tipping point but we currently remain in a struggle between those who seek power for power's sake and those who seek personal power for the ability to execute their purpose for being on Earth at this time.

There is an understanding that momentum needs to be built on the new energy, that there needs to be movement of healing and plowing forward through any debris left behind on Earth by non-magnanimous politicians who are playing games.

My guides predicted: "The snow will melt as spring opens up and the sun begins to shine again with new powers in Washington."

"I wonder when this will happen," I thought.

Then I heard about the next president. Biden has the power of his son behind him from the Spirit realm, and he has the steely power to forge through the politics of the moment. He has steel in this spine. He directs his anger through that steel and has strong intentions and acts in accordance with them.

"On the other side, the outgoing president (whose name we will not mention again), is a wobbly energy like a bowl of jelly. He is not even a bear to be poked. He is a ball of jelly. As it is touched, it jiggles and creates internal struggle. The emotional self within this man is undirected, reverberated within his heart, his mind, his gut, and has no direct way of creating positivity or action that is fruitful. He has spent his whole life being propped up from the outside. He is like a column of jelly with staves surrounding him of family, political proponents, regular people who see him as powerful. They are seeing their own power in him, not his power — projections onto a political leader by those who are not willing to look within and find the power within themselves, who have grievances of their own. Even though this man is a grievance machine, he is seen as successful. People are only seeing an image of success. This is what he projects."

I wondered, "How can a man who is so jellylike in his being be powerful?"

"Now, we have spoken before that all major political powers on the field today have been in the lost city of Atlantis. Many are completing their soul's purpose that began with the conflicts in that civilization."

There is much being discovered about the previous phases of civilizations by archeologists and geologists. My intuition tells me that the conflicts occurring on Earth today are connected to those that precipitated or occurred at the time of the sinking of Atlantis, and that the current Age of Aquarius is ushering in wisdom that was partially lost all those years ago.

I noticed one manifestation of this in the world of design. As we moved into the twenty-first century, a new color scheme in advertising and product design was introduced with the aqua color I called "Atlantean blue" and lime green. These colors are still popular. They are high vibration colors connected to the higher chakras. Recently a mauve color has been introduced that represents a softened version of purple energy of the crown chakra. These are subliminal signs of a spiritual awakening in the world. At least that's how I see it.

I have no more to add to this — I'll leave it as a challenge to those who remember a past life in Atlantis to provide insight into the politics of that period.

Intention to Allow

I believe it is important to pay attention to the thoughts that seem to come from out of the blue. That is how our guides teach and communicate with us. Messages filter down to us in non-rational ways. It's the magic of intuition. Following a random name took me on a thrilling journey out of time and provided one more clue about the beings I am connected with in the Spirit realm.

Q. Do you allow yourself to daydream, let your mind wonder? Or, are you stuck in rational thought? Are you filling your head with other people's thoughts that are presented to you on a platter — your phone or laptop or TV?

Don't get me wrong. The technology we are privileged to have at our disposal is taking us into new worlds. We just need to use discernment. And that's where intuition comes in.

8

BREATH OR DEATH

It is a profound accomplishment to fulfill one's destiny
or to assist another to fulfill their destiny
and to share in the fruits of that labor.

— Jonas

It was an agonizing summer — the summer of 2013 — driving back and forth to doctors' offices, emergency rooms, and specialists. Someone had to tell us what was wrong with Jim. After two months, he still had not had a lung biopsy, the one procedure that would answer the question "what is this?"

The whole thing began that spring as Jim and I were nearing completion on the apartment building in Cleveland. We had purchased it to renovate and fund our dream of retiring to live in a tropical place in the sun. I spent February through April in the all-Black neighborhood, the only white girl walking to the grocery store or gas station across the street. For months I worked with a crew I had met at the local Home Depot. I would begin my days by picking up the crew and taking them for McBreakfasts before heading to the apartment site where I coordinated and worked as the gopher.

One occasion was a true lesson in humility. My plumber kept missing days due to a sinus infection.

"Why don't you get some medication from your doctor?" I inquired.

"I don't have a doctor," he replied. "Can't afford one. I have to sit in emergency for six hours to get a new script. But I have a pharmacist who will give it to me without one."

Today I wonder what that prescription was but I drove him there regardless, before our breakfast stop. I began to understand the struggles of the poor in the US, which previously had been just a flash on the TV screen. It was now in my face.

Jim took over in May, with a promise from me that I would water his tomatoes and greenhouse plants. I was so appreciative that I had such an idyllic place to go home to in Canada. Gratitude seeped through my body and released the fear I did not realize I'd been living with ......

Jim arrived back on the West Coast with a breathing problem. What had begun as a minor dry cough earlier in the month had progressed over the weeks while he fearlessly, tirelessly worked, fixing drywall, plumbing leaks, etc., up and down stairs and ladders. We thought it was just a cold.

He greeted me and Susan, our good friend, at her house in Seattle, where Jim had flown into before we returned to BC together.

"You look so tired. You've lost a lot of weight," Susan observed.

"It was hard work," Jim replied.

Back we went across the border, to our home in the woods that Jim had refused to leave for the majestic views in the downtown condo we had purchased as an investment and which I so crazily desired to live in. He loved the home with the thousand-square-foot studio we had built, the garden we had landscaped with a pond seeded with goldfish we named after movie stars. Marilyn Monroe was my favorite — a creamy white fish that flashed in the moonlight and grew to be the largest in the pond. It was the home we had lovingly brought our cats to from Victoria and, when they died, buried next to the ravine. Then we raised a whole new brood of Pixie-bobs and half-breeds. Two of them passed while I earnestly tried to turn Jim's mind to a life in a condo in the sky. No such luck. He wanted to live till he died in the house on the ravine, surrounded by his furry pals.

BREATHE

Jim came home from his heart doctor after having his breathing checked. Thinking that it was heart failure that had progressed from a minor problem to something more serious, the doctor sent Jim home with a prescription and the proviso that he go to emergency if his breathing didn't begin to open up. It didn't.

One long weekend when the hospital wasn't fully functioning, Jim spent three days being monitored for a supposed fungal infection in his lungs. Then he was sent home with another prescription and another proviso to see a specialist if it didn't clear up in two weeks. It didn't. It became a more fluid cough.

Near the end of August, we readied to drive to see Jim's heart specialist again for a predetermined appointment time. Always being late — "we will have to sit in the waiting room forever anyway" — I took the steering wheel ten minutes later than planned — "I can make up the time by going my special route." Traffic was bad. Panic and guilt began to wash over me. We would be late. Arriving ten minutes after the appointed time, the receptionist announced, "I'm sorry. You're late and the doctor won't be able to see you today."

I pleaded, explained the dire situation that Jim was in. Finally she allowed us into the doctor's office for a quick examination. We were immediately sent downstairs for X-rays. "Tell them to do them now and send them right up." Showing us the X-rays, the doctor pointed to something and said, "You need a lung biopsy. This is not a heart issue."

Three days later I was sitting on a chair next to Jim's hospital bed as the doctors entered with the results.

WHY NOW?

"We're sorry to tell you this. There is no way to sugarcoat it. It is cancer."

I was stunned. The blood left my face. I fumbled with my reading glasses, trying to stuff them into the right compartment in my purse. They wouldn't go in. "What am I thinking?" I dropped my glasses. The newspaper, folded in half and ready for us to share the crossword puzzle, fell to the floor. I stood up and crossed over to the side of Jim's bed. I stood listening to the details about markers on cells — they indicated bowel cancer — the cells from his lungs. We were then given a quick education about metastatic cancer, something I never imagined needing to know about in my whole life.

After the doctors left, I lay next to Jim on the hospital bed. "We never got to go to Paris together," I said to him.

* * *

I was in a panic to get Jim into treatment as soon as possible. We both fought for his life as the days crept by. Two weeks later he was admitted into the cancer hospital and my daily trips began.

"Are you still my girl?" Jim asked me from his bed — probably the most intimate statement of love he had ever expressed to me. Life-wrenching experiences necessitate intimacy.

During the months leading up to the diagnosis, I had sat in bed with him many mornings, deciphering the meaning of his dreams and channeling guidance and clarity for him. It probably helped me more than him.

It became clear to me that he had completed what he had come to do in this life. Jim had spent three years of his late teens in the US Navy, loading bombs onto planes. Jim's love of the military, not so much while he was in it but the romance of a Band of Brothers, was an important thread in his life. Even after leaving the Navy, he had longed to be a part of a Band of Brothers but with a difference — a Band of Brothers who had a common goal of working for good instead of war, while also acknowledging each other's individuality and autonomy. A Band of Brothers without rules of behavior as in the military. Jim had been respected and loved by two groups of people. He had taught sculpture with a small group of art faculty members, who were definitely individualists. Still, they shared the goal of opening young people's minds and encouraging self-expression. Jim's satisfaction came from the support he received from the group of teachers while creating his own sculpture projects for the students. He loved working with his hands and helping students give shape to their ideas. He also belonged to an informal group of twelve men who got together for over thirty-five years. This was Jim's salvation. He could be himself with them, and I know it kept us together during the rockier moments in our marriage. Jim had fulfilled his life's purpose.

Still, dread overshadowed the powerful insights I experienced during that period. When it became clear he would not recover from the cancer and that the end was near, I called his men's group. All the guys trooped over on the ferry to don yellow nylon gowns. They encircled his bed like a cluster of bumblebees and gave him the best send-off they could from a hospital room. They presented him with a CD entitled *Band of Brothers* with all of their soul songs recorded from one of their yearly getaways. Jim's song was "Wandering Aengus," a poem by William Butler Yeats sung by Jolie Holland and accompanied by a slide guitar that transported him back to his roots in Texas. It pierces my heart each time I hear it:

I went out to the hazel wood,

Because a fire was in my head,

And cut and peeled a hazel wand,

And hooked a berry to a thread;

And when white moths were on the wing,

And moth-like stars were flickering out,

I dropped the berry in a stream

And caught a little silver trout.

When I had laid it on the floor

I went to blow the fire a-flame,

But something rustled on the floor,

And someone called me by my name:

It had become a glimmering girl
With apple blossom in her hair
Who called me by my name and ran
And faded through the brightening air.

Though I am old with wandering
Through hollow lands and hilly lands,
I will find out where she has gone,
And kiss her lips and take her hands;
And walk among long dappled grass,
And pluck till time and times are done,
The silver apples of the moon,
The golden apples of the sun.

* * *

From home to the hospital and back again, I had driven for several weeks in a dismal fog of autumn sadness, anxiety, and sometimes no emotion at all. I was drained. But I found one bright spot on these trips. Taking the same route each day, I noticed a stately tree standing tall in the front yard of a little bungalow in a suburban neighborhood. I watched as the tree turned from its summer green into the yellow of autumn, becoming a brilliant golden beacon. I looked for that tree each day — beauty piercing the sadness of the moment.

Driving to the hospital one day that fall, I asked for Jim's angels to be with him. Upon entering Jim's room, I felt the spirit of my grandmother, Noni. They had always been fond of each other but I was surprised to find it was her. I mused that by marrying me, Jim had connected with English history and a sensibility of consideration and politeness that drew him far from the Texan persona imposed by his birthplace.

Another Lesley, our friend and one of Jim's colleagues, was visiting with a homemade breakfast sandwich with sharp cheddar and egg for Jim. "All food tastes like cardboard," he said. I was thankful for the tasty breakfast. Lesley told me that Jim was saying he could see scalloping waves of colors spreading out on the bed sheets. Waving his hands out in front of him, he described the rotating colors: "... pink and purple ... now blue and gold ..." He was beginning the ascent. Or was it just the morphine? No. Everything he spoke of that day related to his life.

My nephew came to say his goodbyes. I have a picture etched in my brain as well as in my iPhoto, taken from behind. Ben sits next to Jim with his arm on Jim's bony back which arches out of his hospital gown. He reminded me of an Auschwitz survivor, nothing left but the curve of a spine barely holding the rest of the body together.

A friend and Buddhist practitioner arrived with a tape of mystical chanting that we played as a spiritual advisor came to say a few final words. He asked if Jim believed in Spirit. Jim replied, "Silver apples of the moon, golden apples of the sun."

As the day progressed, a few phone calls were made to my brother in the East and to another close friend. Then we were alone.

"You know, I was part of the plot. I worked behind the scenes, but I knew what was going on," Jim said with pride, like a general who had orchestrated a successful coup.

I wasn't quite sure what he was referring to. Could it be the Bay of Pigs, when he was at the ready on the aircraft carrier? Or maybe something from another time — the samurai general scheming behind shoji screens?

Later, he stretched his arm out over the side of the bed and stared down past his palm to the floor below, as if viewing a scene from an airplane window.

"What are you seeing?" I asked.

"A game board."

"The game of life," I mused to myself.

"We dodged a lot of bullets, didn't we." A statement, not a question.

I was thinking, "Who is 'we'? What game were we playing?" I didn't ask.

His visions became incomprehensible to me, and I decided not to question him anymore. He was sliding into a world of his own. I was loathe to leave his side, but the nurses urged me to go home and get some sleep; I was oblivious to the meaning of their suggestion. I must have been in complete denial. I got the call an hour and a half later. He had passed forty-five minutes after I left.

I was shattered. I had spent thirty-seven years with one man. We had helped each other on our souls' journeys. As he was dying, I had felt in complete service to his journey, and I feel grateful to have been able to see his magnificent transformation as he opened his heart to many friends and family. I was honored to be a part of his transition back to spirit. I saw it happen before my eyes. I knew he was in complete acceptance of it.

INVITATION TO GRIEVE A LOSS

While Jim was sick and in hospital, people kept saying, "Make sure you look after yourself."

I really had no idea what that meant. I was living in panic and fear most days. Tuning in to the spiritual wisdom of my guides helped me to see that this was the inevitable next step for Jim's spirit. Knowing that he would be moving into the next phase and that his soul would live on gave me some solace. Both the wisdom and the emotional grief lived together in me.

I gave in to the grief for as long as I needed to and allowed myself to know when it was time to move back into life. Anyone experiencing the loss of a loved one needs to know that it is right to trust your own process. It is not something anyone can understand unless they've experienced it themselves.

Seeing a grief counselor was one of the best things I did. I had so many regrets and questions about our relationship. These things needed to be aired so I could come to a place of peace.

Instead of "Take care of yourself," I think now I'd say, "Be good to yourself."

9

THE RECKONING

He who has gone, so we but cherish his memory, abides with us, more potent, nay, more present than the living man.

— Antoine de Saint-Exupéry

THE RECKONING

A few days after his death, Jim came to me in my morning meditation to show me where he was. Ripples of scalloped waves in iridescent colors fanned out towards a horizon — ripples like he had described pouring out in front of him on his hospital bed.

"I'm not ready to go there," I said out loud. I was sitting in my swan chair, my eyes closed in meditation while my mind flowed over expanding waves of energy. My deceased husband was showing me his pathway through the universe, enticing me towards a ball of flashing light.

"Stop." I shook myself alert. It scared the hell out of me. "It's not that time yet. I will see you again, though." I now see this flash of light in the middle of my eye and know that Jim is here with me.

Ted, my boy cat, was also aware of Jim's presence. The evening after Jim's death, Ted sat in the living room staring into space, his head swiveling from spot to spot. With his cat vision, he was seeing many spirits. Perhaps Jim to reassure him, and perhaps his own mother and siblings. In his own way, Ted was getting the gist of the situation with his feline spiritual senses.

The truth I held to my heart was that Jim was there for me. He came to me in a dream when I most needed support. He wrapped his arms around me and told me he loved me. I sank into his tall, strong body, feeling the most ease I have ever allowed myself to experience in my life. Perhaps this is the peace reported by those who have near death experiences. I hung onto the feeling as long as I could.

So began my journey of singlehood, and as the actress Helena Bonham Carter said about a separation, "You break up, you grieve, you get bored of grieving, and then you finally move on." It was my time now. But I was not ready to see that yet. First, I had to grieve the loss.

Before Jim died, I had imagined moving back to one of my hometowns of Toronto or Montréal. I had pictured myself meeting up with a developer and fulfilling a dream I had of building a condo — a design I'd had in my head for many years since seeing an episode of *House Hunters International* about a townhouse that had a courtyard swimming pool in the center of all the rooms. This was all fantasy — an escape from the dismal present of the moment. When the actual death occurred, I fell apart.

"Half of me is not here," I said to myself as I sat in my darkened living room where Jim and I had spent so many evenings watching TV together. I felt like half a person, like half of me was not in that room. I had to reclaim myself.

Years earlier, I had read how two people in a couple connect through all their chakras. When they split up, the energy has nowhere to ground, like electrical wires not yet hooked up to the power box. That explained it. But there was no solace in that knowledge, just a feeling that there was a gaping hole in my life. I fell into that hole for several months.

Pulling myself out took a giant effort. I recalled a scene on a plane when Jim and I were traveling to Houston to visit family — perhaps one of his family members was even dying. We had separate seats, Jim sitting about five rows behind me, both of us on the aisle. A woman was sitting next to me, a very old woman with long grey hair. I noticed her hand. She was wearing an amazing copper ring engraved with what looked like an astrological symbol. Curious, I asked her about it.

"Don't you know about the women of the copper ring?" and this started a conversation. She looked at me and said, "You are special. See, you have a spot right here on your forehead."

"OK," I thought. She was on her way back to her hometown in Mexico. I was intrigued. We talked about spiritual things.

"You know you will do your true work after he is gone," she said, looking back towards Jim's seat.

I really did begin in earnest after he had gone. The truth is, after the grieving, I did many things I had always wanted to do.

One of them living was in a condo in a high-rise tower with a view of sky. I moved into a place on the eleventh floor of a tower on False Creek. I thought I'd only stay for a year, and I was willing to spend the money so that I could relax and be comfortable to start my new life. I set up my meditation table by an east-facing window with a wide-open view all the way across the suburbs to the towers of Metrotown where I had lived for twenty-five years. Below me was a row of bright green trees, ovoid shapes marching along the corridor of the street. They were *my* trees and they grounded me. From my window, I could let my spirit soar into the nothingness of the sky.

But before all that could happen, a monumental task faced me each day. Along with the slow climb out of grief came the overwhelming job of clearing out the accumulation of stuff housed in Jim's studio. At first I ignored it, instead carving out a spot in front of the giant sliding doors that opened onto a view of the lawn spreading down the slope to the treed ravine below. I placed a small desk there, a desk that had lived in a corner of my grandmother's living room when I was a child. It had held envelopes, writing materials, and the daily correspondences written to her by friends and family in Britain. This became my new meditation altar.

From that little altar I had conversations with Jim. He expressed his love for me and also his regrets. These conversations with his spirit seemed to blunt the grief. Knowing he was around was the encouragement I needed to slowly engage with life again.

REVELATIONS

Finally, I had to muster enough energy to start the process of sorting out this space. Jim loved tools and the studio was a testament to this. As I began to look around, I came upon a photograph of the studio from twenty years earlier. It was a shrine to tools. Several work benches housing various professional tools hugged the walls. Three huge empty worktables created out of sheets of plywood lined the center of the space, ready for any project, big or small, that might strike the heart of the artist. But that was not what actually lay in front of me.

Piles of wood offcuts, motors rescued from old tech equipment, items removed from the house during a renovation — essentially all the materiel that could be stuffed into one space, assaulted my eyes. It was overwhelming. I had to squeeze my body sideways to zigzag along the "pathways" that led from one end of the room to the other.

"Why hadn't he cleared this out when he retired?" I thought, exasperated and already exhausted by the work ahead. I had tried to get Jim to begin this task, but he had been more interested in tuning in to music on radio stations from all over the world. He had finally settled on some Texas stations that played roots-country. He reveled in the music of his youth. "To hell with the material world" had been his post-retirement modus operandi.

One Sunday, I had urged Jim to sort through a box of cassette tapes and find a charity that would take them. That one small box was a start — or so I thought. A few days later, I found the tapes tucked away on a shelf in the far corner of his office.

So, it was left to me to disperse the contents of Jim's life to the world. I wasn't sure I could handle it, but I had to begin somewhere. I advertised the large tools online first and then set a date for a garage sale a couple of weeks later, having no idea how I was going to get it together.

Angels arranged it all. Men who were also devotees of the god of tools showed up. On a Saturday, one guy, an artist I didn't know, arrived to buy the wood planer and looked aghast at the job I had ahead of me to get ready for the garage sale.

"Who's going to organize this?"

"I am." This response sent him to his phone. He called a carpenter friend in the film industry. He was free the next day. The two of them showed up on the Sunday and moved everything unrelated to the sale out onto the patio. Then they unearthed all the large tools and set them up on the tables. They walked away with a few bottles of liquor that had been waiting for a special occasion.

So people were willing to help. What a novel idea! I nervously called a sculpture technician Jim had worked with to ask if he'd help by sorting and organizing the small tools for display. He was happy to do it. Friends from Victoria, realizing I was still grieving, offered to help too. On the day of the sale, they caught the early ferry over the Strait of Juan de Fuca to help with the sales while I called out prices.

Lovers of tools lined up to lust after them until, finally, after six garage sales over two months, the place was clear except for the table saw, the story of which I have only just begun to tell!

Once the tools were done, I needed to tackle the office, with its drawers of artwork, drafting materials, art catalogues, and sketches. Late one evening after one of the sales, I ventured into this space hoping to find an old photograph of myself. Instead, I found myself in front of a bookshelf filled with sketchbooks, all lined up in a jagged row. Deciding to look through those, I pulled out a black moleskin journal.

"Oh! This is not a book of sketches! This is a diary." The date at the top of page one corresponded to the year before Jim and I got together. I flipped to the back page — the year we had started seeing each other. I had picked out the only book on the shelf that wasn't filled with sketches for new sculptures. Coincidence? I thought not. The surprise of finding such a diary sent me up the stairs to my living room sofa, where I poured over Jim's version of our early time together.

The words on those pages revealed more than any photographs could have. Very disturbing words of angst and rage were spewed out on the earlier pages. The dissolution of Jim's relationship with his previous girlfriend shocked me. Images came to my mind which I cannot describe. Then came his thoughts on me. I was too young, not worldly enough for him. Not beautiful enough for him. In fact, at one point he called me ugly. He was ten years older than me and really had fit a lot of world experience in those years. But something changed — I became the one he spent his life with. Perhaps I was less demanding than his previous girlfriend and certainly not as bitchy as his first wife, whom I later met on a trip to Los Angeles. He had at least worked through some of his issues before "Lesley" came on the scene. If I'd known any of this then, we would not have spent a lifetime together.

While I was writing this book, my guides stepped in with comments of reassurance. They told me that Jim and I were meant to be together. "Please begin to see yourself as successful. You are a much more worldly girl than you think you are. Jim needed you at the time of his breakup with his secretary girlfriend. Despite his original estimate of you, you were someone he could relax with. You had no ulterior motives."

"Other than catching him," I thought.

Further times of grief brought with them other insights from my guides. Recently, on the morning of a dear friend's assisted death appointment, I received a soothing message from Jonas. He explained to me that my friend's transition back from whence he came would be a smooth transition as all his friends had been called to assist him by lighting a candle at the designated time. This was certainly a different approach to death than we in Western culture are used to. But we all understood that our friend had not wanted to linger in body with a mind that would not be in charge of navigating his life. We all honored his decision and also realized that his family would grieve the loss of his physical presence in their lives.

Jonas then spoke of Jim's transition: "Lesley, you were such a great assistance to Jim's passage as he slipped into his own spirit while his body was still functioning to a degree. As he left his body, he was completely aware of the journey he had been on that day. The decision to leave the hospital and go home when you did was perfect timing for him. It allowed him to release consciousness of your presence or anything of earthly import and raise his spirit up beyond."

"Thank you, Jonas. I felt so guilty about leaving just before his passing. I thought I should have stayed longer and been there. It is a relief to know that."

Invitation to Reach Out

One of the things that struck me after Jim passed was how insulated we had been. We had relied on each other for so much in our lives. Both Jim and I were control freaks who had lots of friends to enjoy life with, but to give over control of anything of serious consequence was not easy.

Without Jim, I was faced with monumental tasks that required me to reach out for help.

It was a humbling experience. I discovered that in circumstances like the loss of a loved one, people are willing to help. Love is extended from the most unexpected places. I have gratitude and appreciation for all the assistance I received from souls, alive and in spirit, to help me through this period of my life.

Q. Do you have trouble reaching out for help when you really need it? It is not a sign of weakness. It is a sign of humanity.

10

GIRLS CONSPIRE

Love is most nearly itself
When here and now cease to matter.

— T. S. Eliot, "East Coker," *The Four Quartets*

We two girls conspired, one propped up on a stool, one leaning on the granite counter in my kitchen, to conjure the spirit of our dearly departed Jim.

We tuned in to connect with him the evening after the memorial service. The service had brought so many old friends across the Strait of Georgia to my home on the edge of the ravine — the home that Jim had said he wanted to live in until he died. Well, he got his wish.

Susan, my very psychic soul sister, asked Jim, "Would you come back again?"

"Yes," he said, replying through Susan.

"Really! Why?" we both chimed. He had had a real struggle, a battle royale inside himself in this just-completed life.

"Because it's so fun!"

We looked at each other. "Is this the Jim that we knew?"

He continued: "I'll come back and be your nephew, and you will be my auntie — my spiritual guide."

"Godmother" went through my head. I was now beginning to understand this concept. I pondered a new lifetime for him with one of my young nieces. "She is the worldly one. She lives in London — a place that would bring the new boy into fortunate circumstances for his life. Money will not be an object this time round."

AND THE BEAT GOES ON ......

REMEMBERING

A few years later, Jonas contributed more to the discussion of family children ......

One night as I entered my office to put my big plush pink sweater in place for my morning meditation, I felt the electric air of spirit opening up. I sat down for a few minutes, thinking about my day-to-day concerns. I had been searching inside myself for some enthusiasm, and so I began to chant. This brought a bubbly energy around my head and torso.

Jonas explained: "There are joyous spirits just waiting to be born, to come back to play on the earth plane. The energy of children abounds."

He then expanded on these thoughts: "There will be six children born into your family — three with one niece, two with your nephew, one with Lauren, the one with the indigo mind power. He will be an architect, a builder unfettered by self-deprecation and self-doubt."

"Hallelujah," I thought. "He'll be able to complete his mission on Earth."

While I'm aware that all souls have choice, I like to imagine that this will come to pass — that "Jim" will come back.

"Your mother will be the littlest girl with your other niece — a sweet, charming, laughing child. Yes," Jonas said as he read my thoughts, "your mother will choose to be with a family of fun to counteract the seriousness of the upbringing she had in this last family."

"None of these children have materialized yet — maybe by the time I finish this book!" I reply in my mind.

"The fence between you and the souls awaiting will be broached and the gate opened soon."

I sat for a few moments, wondering if there were any of Jim's possessions I should save for him in hopes that he would remember this life and stay in touch with his spirit as he grew up.

As I pondered this question, a song flitted through my mind …… "Working My Way Back to You" by The Spinners.

"A song for you, darling."

"Jim! I can feel you here. Oh Jim. I feel your presence."

Answering my query about his possessions, he said, "The cat lamp. You must keep it for me. I will remember it." As Jim spoke, my mind drifted back to the day we purchased the amber-colored glass lamp in a little antique store on one of our trips to Cleveland. Jim had haggled over the price. I didn't understand why he was so adamant about a five-dollar price reduction. It really wasn't necessary. But that was Jim. "Funny," I had thought. When we brought the lamp home, my mother had complained, "How many cats does he need?"

"Typical!" I said to myself, remembering her negative reaction.

I had placed the cat lamp on a black Art Deco dresser, next to several masculine items — an homage to Jim: a bottle of men's cologne; a little round box with a tortoiseshell top, a silver outline of a cruise ship etched into it, which had housed tea in the cabin of some distant relative's traverse across the Atlantic. Also on the dresser sat a burgundy and gold Japanese jewelry box with a ballet dancer that turned and tinkled when it was opened — a gift brought back from one of Jim's Navy tours in Japan. This I am saving for a future niece. But the cat lamp was the piece that dominated this little tableau. Many times, as I lay in bed, my head would jerk sideways to this amber-colored cat, seemingly directed by some other muscular energy in the room, to receive a message from Jim.

"What else, Jim?" I continued.

"My cool sunglasses and my silk tie. The ring with the malachite stone that cracked in half as it flew off your hand onto the concrete floor in the studio — it is for you to keep. It is one of the pair we had made in our first year together. I would like one of the green boxes that you bought in remembrance of me after I died, the big one, to keep my precious things in when I come back into a new life. All children keep precious things — even boys. They keep toys that are precious to them, cards, other boy things." I had bought two faux malachite boxes in which to keep his precious things from this life — the silver link bracelet I had gifted him on our first anniversary, his Jean Paul Gaultier sunglasses that had given him the air of the cool world traveler, the tie he wore to his first major opening at an art museum.

"The watches have no meaning for me, though I did appreciate these gifts. You were my sweetheart for all those years. I would have left you if I didn't love you. I did love you. I wanted to be with you until I died. I loved your presence in my world. I know that it was not exactly what you were looking for all the time, but it was all I could give. Now, another man will give you what he can, and I will thank him for it."

He continued: "Now I live in my powerful spirit. Sometimes powerful spirits need to live 'ordinary lives' to find their way back to their greatness. For, if it is given at birth, it is often squandered. I needed to go through the period in the sixties. I was on the cutting edge of that era. I went from being a hard-nosed critic of the world when I entered the Navy, to being softened by my travels and opening my heart to different cultures — also touching on past lives through my journeys. And then I became the extreme opposite as a crazy-ass artist.

"My struggle was deep. The women before you were necessary. You received me at a time when I was willing and able to take the path towards fulfillment of my life's purpose.

"Now, we, on the other side in spirit, are cheering you on. I particularly am the Emperor to your Empress/Fool in your spiritual endeavors. As you know, you are the Fool — as in the Fool card, new beginnings — for you are just beginning this new adventure as the Empress.

"You have advanced far further than the majority of people you know in your world. You need guidance from us — your Noni is with us, too — Me and Noni and Jonas, who leads us and gives us assignments. You do receive understanding and inclinations to new understanding when you are sleeping.

"It is a positive thing that you are waking up very early in the morning for you are gaining strength from the memories of your dreams. The thing you can remember from today's early dream is that you are a tower of strength — a brick tower like the central image in Brian's painting that hangs in your living room. This is your tower of strength. In the drawing, it is your spirit version of a tower."

At this point I had to go into my living room to look at the drawing

Jim was referring to. The tower is drawn in charcoal and is somewhat transparent, ephemeral.

"This represents your spirit. In your dream, you saw a brick tower — an Earth tower. Together they represent your spiritual power incarnate on the earth plane."

This rang true. I had woken from the dream with a sense of power. The dream held a bit of mystery too.

So Jim was now a spirit guide, helping to pilot my course. I do have a lot of help from the other side — we all do, if only we open ourselves up to the wisdom and don't allow our rational minds and old beliefs to negate it.

War

The next day, my meditation again brought in Jim's energy.

"Jim … Oh, Jim …"

"You will only understand the true nature of my life in respect to my need to shed all the negative things that I have done in past lives with my warlike energy — the masculine energy that needs to prove itself in war."

He continued: "Now, there have been powerful, positive aspects to wars — the movement of philosophies, the movement of goods, the connection of peoples of different cultures — and definitely the connection between West and East."

This message from Jim reminds me that he had spent many hours, with my great admiration, reading the full twelve-volume collection of Arnold Toynbee's *A Study of History* and many other in-depth historical treatises. I was amazed at his power of concentration, reading books that outlined history in such great detail. I have never had the patience to pore over the past so meticulously. I often turned to Jim for context when I encountered details of another lifetime for myself or any of my clients.

Jim's historical interests leaned towards war and action movies — *Gladiator* was of particular interest to him. I'm sure he had a lifetime as a fighter in the Colosseum. His interest in these things opened my eyes to the cruelty of ancient Rome. It also led me to tap into a scene of a past life that I was to re-encounter in a future relationship. But this came later ......

JONAS ON JIM

Another day, while meditating, Jonas speaks to me of Jim ...

"Now, we will go back to Jim, who has a much more priestly presence now, as he has gained much acclaim for his power to overcome his aggressive masculine tendencies and live through his feminine tendencies of creativity and mysticism in appreciation of the arts.

"So just as you, as a woman, needed to learn to bring out the masculine aspect in yourself, so did he, as a very masculine man, need to bring the feminine aspect to flourish in the world. He believed in himself intrinsically, although he had difficulty expressing that in the world. For being highly feminized in his interests in the arts, there was a reticence to expose this in a masculine world. This was a reason for him to grow up in Texas and create the move for himself to Canada, where feminine aspects are more appreciated — the heart above the gun. He found a great home in your support, in your love, and in his power as a teacher and proponent of delving deeply into personal talent, which he encouraged in his students. The ones who could see his depth and his power within were those he connected with most strongly. He came up in a generation where male and female were very separate. But the men and women he taught came into a world where the combination of male and female aspects within the individual is acceptable and desirable.

"You gave him a beautiful sense of peace despite the anger and resentment he expressed towards his early life. Underlying your relationship was a true supporting of each other's powerful path and purpose in the lifetime that you shared together. He is now supporting you from a place of peace and integration of all understanding so that he is as a priest in his own right, with both male and female aspects. You see, in the spirit world, it is just love and intelligence combined as opposed to male or female ... Love and wisdom ... Now, you see Jim in your mind as masculine because that is how he expressed himself physically in the world. He did live many, many lifetimes as a man, as you have lived many, many lifetimes as a woman trying to express your power, the power of female that was thwarted so many times. He is now here to help to enhance your female aspect, for his love of you was of the female that is your essence. The beauty he saw in you was greatly enhanced by his support. And he was well aware of how he was a support for you even if he did not express it outwardly. He so truly wishes to be back in your life again in a new way, holding you dearly as the mystic that you are ......"

ENCOURAGEMENT

Jonas continued: "I know that you had pain in your life, the little hurts, the little darts that were only indicative of a bigger pain —the biggest pain was the pain of being your true self in a world gone mad with power. So, as you were assisting Jim with his search for a Band of Brothers who were not warriors, you were assisting yourself as well to grow out of the madness of the hunt for power and to grow into the beautiful woman of deep and spiritual understanding that you always have been.

"Particularly in this lifetime, you know you're worthy of love. Your lover Jim brought you to a new place to love yourself. At the end, he realized how important you were in his life. He had a deep love and affection for you, for who you are and who you were to become."

GEMS BEFORE, GEMS AFTER

Jonas spoke of the gems of support in my life …

"All right. We are giving you a little pep talk about money now. We created for you a man of great wealth and wisdom to be part of your cadre of souls in this lifetime — 'cadre' meaning a small group of souls trained in the spiritual arts, supporters of yours. You have always been the center of this circle of souls incarnated.

"Jim … Jim was the man of great wealth of understanding and clarity about what he wanted in life. He provided you with the platform upon which you could shine. He held you up for all to admire, to be born into this new woman — priestess — that you are becoming. You are live. You are live now, Lesley. You are going live. Your home now is on the internet. You are creating that for yourself at this time.

"You need only look to the beautiful gems laid out before you on your table — or shall we call it an altar? — to see where all the wealth came from. The wealth of all the souls who supported you all your life are represented there."

On my altar I have placed rings with diamonds, sapphires, and other beautiful gemstones, as well as gold bracelets that I inherited from all the women in my family. It gives me a sense of connection to the earlier generations and honors their contributions to the world.

"Know that all these souls come together in support of you. And that your Noni calls them all in when necessary. Of course, all these souls were guided by myself, Jonas — I have been the steadfast leader of the pack. I am now joined by Jim. We two are great friends."

"Really?"

"Yes. Jim incarnated to be with you on this journey in life. Your next man will be the finishing touch, the icing on the cake. But Jim baked the cake. And you ..."

"Of course, I was the ingredients."

The whole group of guides seemed to be participating in this discussion: "Jim came to you at the perfect time. His ego was not attracted to you at first, but his golden soul was attracted to the golden being within you. Now, we want to tell you that there was a discussion between Jonas and Jim about who would incarnate ..."

"Ohhh ... Oh my God," I gasped, chills flooding my body. The discussion was a revelation and filled my body with an energetic charge. "I really feel it in my solar plexus!"

"... who would incarnate to be with you again. It was decided that Jim, having been the laborer in Egypt, needed to take on the role of supporter to the princess/priestess, whereas I, Jonas, have already been your supporter in other lifetimes."

I felt the power of these statements as I sat cross-legged in my swan chair. Flashes of time periods, like a kaleidoscope of slides swiftly changing, floated before the screen of my inner eye. A lush Egyptian valley in the shadow of the temple transformed into a group of men in flowing robes following Jesus in a dry desert. The tinkling of delicate sake cups behind a shoji screen all blended together into iridescent light. Veils of time were being lifted, and I was immersed in the energy of the Universal Force.

The spirits continued: "Jonas and Jim are now chuckling, clinking beer glasses, metaphorically speaking, in the world of spirit. Many mansions. Your golden throne awaits you, our darling. You will indeed spend time in London Town, for the DNA within you is drawing you back to your roots in the medieval times, in the Roman times, in the Egyptian times. You will find a way to live in London. There will be no need to worry about money. Ten times ten times ten is a million. Revive this mantra you used to say." These words floated through my head, reminding me that there are no limits. "It will be the gift of the gods to you as you fulfill your message of help to the world. Great things are coming into the world for those who are smiled upon, those who learn of their soul's purpose, those who know that they are spirit as well as body. All others will need to refer back to the Spirit world for further instructions, but it is all in hand. The hand of God loves all and gives all that is needed to bring all back to pure love. Amen."

"Oh my goodness, oh my goodness."

"These are but a few of the souls, of the spirits who await this book. There are many that you will reach up to in the coming months. The Bells are ready for your awakening. Amen.

"All is in hand, ready to be distributed to the speech and the powerful incantations that will come forth from your mind between God and you.

"Henceforth and forevermore, when on earth and in sky you will walk with the Giants of Love and Light."

INVITATION TO LIVE YOUR TRUE SELF

This channeling was a powerful shift in my energy. The use of religious terms to describe the Universe or Spirit resonated deeply with me. I hear these words in the context of ancient spiritual practice, as metaphor and not as the limitations that are inferred by our earthly religions today or as they were used to control the masses in the past. I am becoming more and more aware of the multiplicity of spiritual experiences that make up the true me. I am being challenged to share that with the world.

We all have parts of ourselves we don't want to show the world. Both my husband and I have struggled to expose our true selves to the world. Jim, a talented artist, was always nervous about how his work would be received, and so he wasn't able to fully appreciate his successes. I, as you know, have held back my true knowing from anyone I thought would be critical of me. I have challenged myself to work through this and am beginning to love myself more and more.

We are in an era when we are all being challenged to awaken to our own truth, our own beauty, our own talents, and our inner power. The world needs us to do this. We all have a contribution to make. Let us be in our magnificence as spirits walking the earth plane.

Q. Do you have the courage to embrace the magnificent uniqueness that is you? Can you allow yourself to be and do what you want for a whole day? How about two whole days?

Perhaps if you do this enough, you will find you enjoy life more and make it a habit to be true to yourself every day.

II
POWER

WAVES OF TIME

The waves crash on the shore

And brush the sands of time

Perpetuate the life

That the sands hold within

Each grain of sand is like a universe

Enabling the viewer to see

The potential within themselves

For envisioning a future

Built on wisdom from the past.

11

BOMBS BURST AROUND ME

History doesn't repeat itself, but it often rhymes.
— Mark Twain (attributed)

BEGIN ANEW

Although the passing of my soulmate Jim was the major transition of my life, I did not write this book to focus on recovering from the grief of losing someone that I loved. I leave that to others who have experience in grief counseling.

Instead, my goal is to help others recognize that we all have connections through many lifetimes with many people. It is exciting to experience and understand those centuries-long relationships, as I have done through my channeling with Jonas and other magnificent spirits. Jim drew on his own idealism to help me move forward with love and passion on our path together. Once he passed to the other side, our relationship across the veil became the catalyst to me recognizing my *own* power as a spiritual being.

Once the grief let go of its hold on me, I needed to create a life as a single woman. To do this, I had to go inward.

Continuing with my spiritual practice, I realized there were more past life connections to be revealed. I was drawn to attend a past life regression presentation at a midsummer fair in Vancouver. I went in thinking I would discover more about my Egyptian lifetime but — surprise, surprise — this was not what came up on my mind screen.

A Reveal

Bombs burst around me. The buzz of planes overhead made my blood run cold as my legs took me to safety as fast as they could. Tanks began to rumble on the edge of town, and people all around me screamed and scrambled over the rubble. Sirens shrieked — woo-ee, woo-ee. The entire town was being carpeted with bombs. Smoke and debris filled the air. Then, nothing. I floated upward in a cloud of peace as my body went down. It was the end. No more running. No more fear. No more humiliation. No more following orders I didn't want to fulfill. It was over.

I looked back at the fractious scene, and the pain of my broken heart released as I spoke the words, "I am sorry. I am sorry I left you. I am sorry I put myself ahead of my love for you. Can you forgive me? I was only trying to survive, live through the nightmare of being a soldier in Germany. Being with you would have drawn attention to you. Your father asked me to leave. He wanted a chance to save you and your family, and I would have jeopardized your escape from this hell. But for me, it all came to this end anyway."

"Slowly open your eyes." There I was again, sitting in a room with a group of people. I had followed the suggestion of the leader as she asked us to go to the lifetime that was still unconsciously affecting this present life deeply. As we all emerged from our visions, she instructed, "Ask yourself what the main outcome was of the lifetime you just experienced."

My first thought was … "There are no dragons to slay."

"What does that mean?" I pondered.

The answer floated into my mind … "All activity in the world is a construct of the human, earth-bound mind. It is a play created by us and for us for our edification and entertainment while on Earth."

My next thought … "I will never again follow the beliefs of a leader who wants to subvert the will of the individual. I will look to my own inner guidance, my own mind, for direction. This is one clue as to why I have never wanted to join in, to join clubs, organizations, religions that have a code of ethics or set of beliefs that must be followed to be accepted."

In the past I had watched many TV shows about Germany and the Second World War. I was searching for an explanation for how Hitler was able to transform the country and make people follow him. For how he turned the minds of the citizens towards hate and destruction. The past life regression had given me a taste of the fear and fervor that had permeated Germany at that time.

Germany Rears Its Head Today

Journal note, August 2020: I am furious this evening!

As I cleaned up my kitchen, I listened to a newscast. It was about what the Trump government was doing to restrict voting in the 2020 presidential election by interfering with the post office. The further into detail the newscast went, the more agitated I became. Even though I don't live in the US, I asked myself, "What is going on?" The discomfort in my belly turned to rage — fury. I have within me the memory of the same sort of tactics of restriction being used in Germany to bolster the power of Hitler.

How could this be happening in the democratic nation that is our neighbor to the south? Trump seemed to be reading directly from Hitler's playbook, taking advantage of the country's dire financial situation during the pandemic. But unlike Germany, whose economic problems were the result of the reparations levied against it from the Allied Powers after World War I, this president appeared determined to undermine the economy from the inside. Although he said he was not, by ignoring the coronavirus and caring nothing about the people disadvantaged financially, he was creating the same conditions of hatred and fear that were crafted by the Nazis under Hitler's power.

My radar was buzzing so loud it was hard to ignore it and be grateful for the safe existence I led. The memory of my last lifetime had ignited my nerve endings once again.

Let us not rhyme this history. Let us write a modern poem — one that does not rhyme.

The winds of time blow as eddies and gusts
Forming patterns of energy
Flowing within the consciousness.
The wealth of nations flows
In concert with the gusts and creates
Hurricanes of dust.
The hope of nations will again be changed,
Transforming into calm seas
Of literature and words of praise.

The arms of the gods will hold on to those
Who fly with the energy of this charge.
The hopes and dreams of past have been obliterated
And mix in the cauldron for a new elixir
Of proud momentum into the sunshine
Of the world's peaceful transformation.

Of course, Jonas had much to add on the topic of Germany and the world today …

"OK. Many sparks and clashes of energy are blowing up old ideas and bringing out the naysayers whose essential message is 'We do not want to change.' Throughout history, when a new political or religious movement takes hold, there are groups of people wanting to maintain the status quo and others wanting to move into the new. Now, in the globalized world we live in, there are many groups, white nationalists and others, who are fighting the change of opening up the world to an energy of peace and accommodation of different cultures within the whole. It is the challenge of your time."

Jonas continued: "Some of the people alive today were Jews during the Holocaust. Some, who were Nazis, are continuing the fight, still carrying the torch to eliminate the Jews. In their minds they are doing right. They are trying to achieve the stability that Trump has promised them.

"There can be great animosity that bleeds through the consciousness from other lifetimes. World War II created much to be contemplated. Many present lives are filtered through a lifetime during that war. It is an age-old problem of humanity — the inability to change, the inability to accept new ideas. The aggravation and rage of World

War II is expanding into the world again. It has only been seventy years. You on Earth are still playing, metaphorically speaking, in the fields plowed by that war.

"After the war, the baby boomers flourished on the societal platform that their parents had created, and they envisioned a new peaceful world. Many came out of the ashes of the Second World War to right the wrongs of their lifetimes then.

"You will see that many of the people drawn to you in past life regressions will have had a lifetime in that war. That is your era to heal. You will find the need is great in this area within the Jewish people. Some souls who were not Jews in a past life are now drawn to become Jewish to right the wrongs of the war."

GENERATIONAL ZEITGEIST

Jonas continued: "Now, you yourself are on the cusp of a new energy which brings you fear due to your German experience — the question of whether to speak out or keep quiet. You are not the only one. But you are all waking up again to the fact that, in the world today, you must speak out and live in your truth."

I asked myself, "So why, after all that has been revealed about my last lifetime, am I still afraid to speak out about my spiritual understanding with family and friends?" I knew it was partly about my family's reaction, but it seemed bigger than that. My last lifetime in Germany had impacted me as well, but that was not enough to shut me down completely. Why did I have such trouble voicing my opinion in the greater world? I am fascinated by politics but afraid to join in any protests for fear of reprisals.

INVITATION TO JOURNAL

Once I decided to write a book, I became nervous about exposing myself. This past life regression I participated in revealed one of the reasons for this fear. I had long been interested in wartime Germany, but this experience explained the deeply personal reason why it was a time period and place that was still affecting this lifetime in a negative way. Knowing something intellectually and feeling it are two different things. But, what I learned has helped diminish my fears of being myself and speaking out.

My interest in understanding the German experience of World War II helped me learn a great deal about my fears in my current life. In the same way, your personal interests could be clues to other lifetimes that you have led. For instance, a friend of mine recently told me that her son speaks fluent Japanese. No one in her family is Japanese, and her son has red hair like her. I asked her how he became interested in learning Japanese as a teenager. She said that, as a child, he loved Japanese cartoons, and that set him on the path. At university he was able to enjoy the friendship of both Canadian and Japanese students and acted as a translator between the two. She wasn't surprised when I said he must have been Japanese in a past life.

Prompt:

I am drawn to the time period in the past when ......

If I could choose another time or place to live a life, it would be ......

The details that draw me to that are ......

12

PLENTY OF MEN, BUT...

Love is something sent from heaven
to worry the hell out of you.
— Dolly Parton

READY FOR LOVE

My story has now caught up to the book's opening scene on the steps of the temple.

I had finished clearing out Jim's studio with the exception of the fated table saw. I had done enough grieving, at least for the time being, when a gorgeous blue-eyed man, Leo, arrived at my front door to pick up the last of Jim's tools — the table saw.

For several years before he had passed, Jim had wanted us to move back to Victoria, but I had resisted. Now he seemed to be an actor in this play, sending me a man from Victoria who was not only determined to buy Jim's saw but looked at me directly in the eye and commiserated with me about the loss of my husband. We joked that the saw was going back to its original home. I could tell he was interested in me. Leo drove away with the saw but we kept in touch over emails.

Leo was a most intriguing candidate for a new relationship. As I asked, "Have I known this man before?" a shocking scene played in my mind's eye and assaulted my sense of dignity. The vision of leaving Leo behind as I ran out of the temple — because, yes, it was he who had been my lover in Egypt — was not the only scene that convinced me that Leo could be the next man in my life.

Out of the blue, another answer flashed — "Gladiator, Roman." I pictured a Roman man wearing what looked like a slatted skirt, part of a gladiator or soldier's armor, I didn't know which. Searching for more …… "Oh my God! How could this be! How could this be!" I shuddered. "This is even worse …"

I am in the stands of the Colosseum. The crowd roars. The acrid smell of blood and revenge is in the air and jealousy sits next to me in the form of my mother. In the scene on the contest floor, dust flies up from under the gladiator's feet as he draws back his sword and plunges it into the sweaty chest of the limp and exhausted Christian. I am resplendent with joy. "He is mine now!" Or more to the point, I am his, for my father has pledged me to the winner of this combat, knowing full well that the Christian had no hope of survival.

I pulled out of this scene in shock. The reality slowly sunk in. I had been a pawn in the game of Roman politics. "Oh my God. This is disastrous. This explains a lot. No wonder I am attracted to this guy. And I've invited him into my house."

I had seen this scene before but never the ending and certainly not the contestants in the fight. Sitting next to me in the stands of the Colosseum was Kitty, my teacher from this life. I was the beautiful young daughter with long flowing hair and bejeweled neckline and hairpiece, seated next to the older, jealous mother who was married to one of the aristocrats of the time, my father. During an earlier meditation session, I had felt the rancor and jealousy of my mother reflected for a brief moment in the eyes of my teacher, Kitty, not knowing what it was about at the time. But as I witnessed the entire scene with Leo as the blue-eyed victor, it all made perfect sense.

As shocked as I was at this memory, I felt that a romantic relationship was sure to develop between Leo and me — there were so many connections. We kept up the correspondence over email, back and forth, back and forth, sending musical links. "Shine On You Crazy Diamond" by Pink Floyd sent me to sleep many nights and also sent me back to being fourteen years old. I was thrilled. This was the new man of my dreams.

Jim seemed to be an orchestrator in this scheme. One day as Leo and I sat eating lunch at his kitchen table, Jim flashed over his shoulder. "That was interesting," I thought. But I got the vibe that Leo wasn't interested in a romance with me. The internet was awash in advice about getting out of the "friend zone." I binged and I plotted, but to no avail. Despondent about the situation, my heart was in my throat many times when I talked to him.

How Will This End?

During one of my weekend trips to Victoria, Leo announced to me, "You know, the girlfriend I had in Australia would iron naked."

God, if that wasn't an off switch to my hopes for making it happen with this man. You wouldn't catch me dead swanning around naked doing housework. I wasn't really happy with my own naked body at the time and hadn't been naked with another man besides Jim for many years. Let's just say this was not the first hint that a romantic relationship was not in the cards with this man. But what of the time I saw Jim over Leo's shoulder while we sat at his kitchen table? Wasn't that a good sign? Were we really just meant to be friends? What about him being my lover in Egypt? This couldn't be the end.

I turned to my friend Sootara to moan about this situation. I couldn't let go of this guy. She told me that I could change the outcome of the past life by reimagining the vision and changing the ending. By doing this, maybe I could change the way I felt in the present.

I quieted myself and, in my mind, I saw myself running down the steps of the temple. I turned to see Leo waiting there for me. This time I ran up to him and kissed him goodbye before leaving. This dampened my ardor for him somewhat. I began to recognize that he was sent to me to help me heal, find the fourteen-year-old girl in me again, moon over love songs, and fuss with my makeup. The realization was sad but liberating.

In the meantime, Leo shared with me his Plenty of Fish profile — his way of letting me down easy by describing the woman identical to the Australian girlfriend he'd left behind. My heart was still pining for him although I knew it was hopeless. Why hadn't he gone back to Australia to be with his naked, beautiful blonde? Why was he still looking for her on Plenty of Fish in Canada? Why he didn't go back to her, the love of his life, was beyond me. But I was beginning to see that this man did not have what it takes to be in touch with his own power and his own life direction.

At this point, I decided to help him get back into his chosen career as helicopter pilot and so lined up a date in Vancouver. I told him to set up a meeting with the head of the helicopter company he had previously worked for and then take me out for a birthday lunch, which he did. He got the job. I knew I was meant to be there to assist him in pulling his life back together, just as he had helped reawaken the girl in me.

Still, I never really gave up on romance with Leo until an old friend came back into my life to fill in more information about that Egyptian lifetime.

New Year's Hope

I arrived home from a Toronto Christmas trip with family just in time to spend my first New Year's Eve alone. It was time to go on Plenty of Fish. I wrote out my profile and posted. Ten minutes later, I got hits from several men. Wow — there are lots of desperate guys looking to get laid on New Year's Eve. Booty-call night! One in particular was very aggressive and lived near me. He wanted to date that night. It was 10:45 p.m. "No way!" He had a heavy accent which gave me creepy visions of my European boyfriend at university who had wanted to do acrobatic sex — not my scene. Not interested in meeting this guy.

I persisted with Plenty of Fish for several weeks and several one-shot coffee dates, still holding out hope that Leo would awaken to my beauty.

This was the unpromising beginning of my search for a new man who had at least a modicum of spirituality — SBNR, spiritual but not religious.

The next man was an artist — a definite contender. His first question was "What are you wearing?" That should've been a sign to just hang up. I wasn't that desperate, but I persisted with a conversation and actually met him for a coffee date. He showed up in a pair of jeans, a white shirt, casual jacket, and a silver skull ring on his finger. My gut told me this guy was trouble, and I cut him loose.

Next was a man who lived south of the border in Bellingham but had an ex and a son living in Vancouver. He fantasized about me as the beautiful woman by his side — he in his kilt, me in some tartan gown at his next regimental dinner. I do have Scottish heritage, but I haven't worn tartan since my grade-nine school uniform.

There were several other coffee dates with different men. I recall I had eight but can only account for five in my memory. Then there were the emails: "Hi" from Florida, "How are you?" from New York. I even attracted attention from some guy in London. Don't these people have anything better going on in their lives?

Nearing the end of my rope, a guy got my attention with tickets to a Lady Gaga concert. We agreed to meet at a local breakfast café. Seated in a booth, I watched him come towards me — a man dressed nicely in a crisp cotton shirt and jeans — an upgrade, to my eye, from the tees and sweatshirts worn by everyone else as the urban uniform in Vancouver. As we began to talk, I noticed that he wore several gold and diamond rings on his fingers which then darted out at me when he made a point. It was difficult not to blink and show alarm at these intrusions into my facial space. No concert tickets could persuade me he was the guy for me.

The final date was Captain Bill. He fit me in one day after completing his real estate exam. He owned a yacht and had lost his girlfriend to cancer; she had been his partner for the harbor tours he led. He was obviously looking for a new model. I obviously was not it. This was apparent as he manipulated me into paying for my own lunch. Yet, as we were saying goodbye at the curb, he said, "Well, aren't you at least going to give me a little tit," waited for a hug, gave me a quick frontal bump, and then turned and walked away. That was the last straw.

Every one of these men was different but had one thing in common. They all had an ideal woman in mind — a projection of their needs. I wasn't interested in becoming someone's other half. Or maybe I was the one who had an ideal man in mind. If I did, none of them came close.

During this period, I binged on videos about how to get out of the friend zone — I still had Leo in mind — how to appeal to a man, how to make him interested. I did learn one valuable thing: men, first and foremost, want to be respected. Love comes second. This gave me something to ponder in regards to the frustrations I'd had with Jim. "Maybe if I'd been more …?"

Looking back, I marvel that Jim and I found each other in all the world. We had both been drawn to the small city of Victoria, Jim from Texas with grandparents from Italy and Germany, me, a Scottish, English, Welsh descendent of people who had crossed the Atlantic for better lives. And we had seemed perfectly made for each other.

I wasn't willing to spare any more time on the endeavor of online dating. There are plenty of fish in the sea, but not the one I wanted. I would quit the website, taking my chances that I would meet the right person for me just by living my daily life. I'd leave my fate to the gods.

The following week, magic happened.

INVITATION TO WRITE

Embracing the hope of finding a new partner, I learned a lot by putting myself out there:

Number one — physical appearance and sexual attraction do not always make for a good relationship.

Number two — past life connection does not always need to be re-engaged even if it brings up intense feelings.

Number three — I need someone who hits on all four areas: physical, emotional, mental, *and* spiritual.

After being with a man who fulfilled all these aspects, I was willing to wait for the next guy. I knew he wouldn't be the same as Jim. I wasn't looking for that. I wasn't the same woman. I was looking for someone I could connect with as the new person I was.

Prompt:

The qualities I am looking for in a partner are ......

13

OLD ME, NEW ME

All our dreams can come true,
if we have the courage to pursue them.

— Walt Disney

INTO THE FUTURE

"What are your plans for the future?" he asked. "Where do you want to settle?"

"I'm thinking of Honduras. There's a development there in the north, on the ocean, where you can buy a property and choose a house design option, which includes a pool, hot tub, and all the modern conveniences, from $100,000 to $200,000, so the total cost would be maximum $300,000."

Leo had told me about this environmentally friendly community being built in an area that was great for diving and snorkeling. It sounded ideal to me. I could live there mortgage-free if I sold my house.

"Honduras! Don't you know it's the murder capital of the world!"

"Oh! … OK … So what are your plans?"

"Well … I'm thinking about Panama. You can live very well there on $1,500 a month. It's listed by *International Living Magazine* as one of the best places to retire in the world."

This was how the conversation began on the day I met the next man on my journey. I had been invited to lunch by an old friend from Victoria ……

Let me go back to the time after Jim had passed. I was still meandering over details of my life with my husband and at the same time was perplexed by the response I was getting from Leo. I was trying to figure out my relationship to men.

One day, I was seated at my little meditation table, set up in front of the plate glass sliding door of the large studio that had been converted from a carport for Jim. It was an obvious spot for me to filter through my memories and connect with Jim's spirit.

I had a burning desire to understand something Jim had done before he died. I called an old friend from Victoria who had been in Jim's men's group. Surely he would help. The answer was not forthcoming. But Rob did ask me if I'd be interested in going to a lunch in Vancouver that he was arranging with our mutual friend, Wolf, to meet his — Rob's — new love.

"Sure. That would be great."

I hadn't known that Wolf was living in Vancouver or that he had separated from his wife. I was intrigued and a little bit amused at myself for being drawn to make this call at this particular time. This seemingly innocent phone call became the start of something new but was also, as I later discovered, karmic.

The day of the lunch, I had arrived at the Granville Island restaurant early and decided to wander around for a while. Passing by shops displaying beautiful wares handcrafted by local artisans, I glimpsed a man who I guessed was Wolf. He had on a poncho and a skull cap and seemed to be skulking around as if he was awkward in this place. I quickly turned away so I wasn't seen. By the time I arrived at the restaurant, the three were already seated at the table next to the fireplace on the outdoor terrace. And there was Wolf in a different guise — the southern gentlemen who stood up, pulled out my chair, and placed a blanket on my shoulders as I sat down.

"Hmmm … This is nice. Nice to be treated this way," went through my mind. And so I had met another potential soulmate.

* * *

I drove Wolf to the bus stop with the farewell of "We'll get together again soon." I didn't contact him for a few weeks. There was something inevitable about this meeting, but I was not in a rush to move it forward — a very different stance for me to take with a man I was interested in. For one thing, he had become a rabbi! I wasn't sure if this would work. But, it could also be interesting.

After spending a few days digesting what I had learned at a workshop on presentation techniques I had attended one weekend, I felt ready to engage with a new man and called to see if Wolf wanted to meet. He was interested. We settled on a movie — *Woman in Gold*, coincidentally about a Jewish woman trying to recover a family painting stolen by the Nazis. Confirming the day before, Wolf asked if I'd be OK going to a music event instead. "The person I teach bar mitzvah classes with is giving a small concert in a café on Main Street."

"Sure," I replied, just wanting to find some common interest.

The singer was beautiful. She'd written her own songs. Wolf and I sat crowded on a bench next to each other, enjoying the music and the atmosphere. Nearing the end of the evening, he put his hand on my thigh, and that was the sign. He liked me.

How had we come together after all these years? And ... it happened only a week after I took down my Plenty of Fish profile.

KISMET

Wolf and I had first met thirty years earlier in a therapy group. That night on our first date after so many years had passed, we talked about our past connection in that group. I had really liked him back then and had invited him to my place after walking home from group, making him an omelet in my tiny kitchen. He had expressed surprise that I had so little food in my fridge — a jar of mustard, a sweet potato, and a dozen eggs, maybe some cream ... I continued to explain how I had been frustrated while trying to connect with him in a pub one night years ago, feeling his quiet behavior was a sign that he was judging me. I had taken it as a rejection. He remembered none of it. He had made an impression on me, but apparently I hadn't made much of an impression on him. Wolf had gone on to marry someone else and so did I.

I lost my husband, and he divorced his wife around the same time. We were in sync for meeting again.

When I called my friend and told her I was seeing someone new and that he was a rabbi, she laughed.

"You're *schtupping* a rabbi!" she exclaimed in her irreverent manner.

I laughed at her humorous use of a Yiddish expression. It was strange introducing my friends and family to my rabbi lover. He was so different from the Waspy upbringing my friends and I were immersed in. As time went on, I realized that the Jewish faith, at least the version Wolf subscribed to, could be quite a bit more liberal than many forms of Christianity. There is no body shaming, no focus on sin, which Wolf explained was a Christian construct. Rather, it has a set of practices and rituals that lead to a good and happy life. Women can become rabbis, and there doesn't appear to be prejudice against LGBTQ, at least in the most modern form of Judaism. Many of the members of his synagogue participated in the pride parade each year, wearing rainbow colors in support. The images of Hasidic Jews I had associated with Judaism is only one version, and the most conservative. That was not Wolf.

We had a lot more in common than our religious roots. We talked about music. I told him about the song my dad had sent me the day he died. He expressed interest. "Benny Goodman was Jewish, you know." So began the conversation of the considerable influence the Jews have made on American culture.

On our second date, we had dinner in one of the many new vegetarian restaurants in Vancouver. That evening, my dad sent me the song "And the Angels Sing" once again. This new relationship was meant to be.

An early morning meditation confirmed it. I sat in an atmosphere of loving energy when Jonas, my guardian angel, spoke: "You two have been together all your life. You each had to live an earthly life before you could come back together. Wolf had a family and you, a wonderful marriage filled with much love and creativity, which propelled your souls forward. And now you've come together to continue your souls' purposes." I knew/felt this to be true. We had known each other in spirit all along.

Leaving his apartment one afternoon, skipping down the stairs we broke out in song — Frank Sinatra's "Young at Heart," covered recently by Cyrille Aimee, a beautiful French jazz singer.

"That's a real oldie. Not from my time. How do I know all the words to these songs?" Wolf said with astonishment.

"Well, I know them because my dad played all the big band music. You must have been steeped in the jazz standards when you lived in New Orleans."

Jazz became our date night out. I loved it.

Wolf introduced me to the musical chanting of the Jewish service. He told me about Rabbi Shlomo Carlebach, a musician he admired who had written a chant which Wolf sang to me. The next day, I sat to meditate and began chanting my usual OHM when the Rabbi's tune emanated from my lips with new words — "I am the world, I am the man, I am the woman in thee." "I" seemed to reply in the same up and down tune — "you are the world, you are the man, you are the woman in me." It was a mind-altering meditation on the connection between myself and spirit.

This certainly was an interesting new relationship I had on my hands!

GLEAMING WHITE TOWERS

In the first little while when Wolf and I were getting to know each other, I lived on the eleventh floor of a condo tower at the end of False Creek. My windows afforded me wonderful nighttime views of the city lights and the rotating colors of the sports arena and the geodesic dome of Science World, sparkling and enlivening my world.

Walking along the waterfront one day, with the scene of the three white towers where I lived in the distance ahead of us, I said to Wolf, "I love this scene."

"What about it do you like?" he asked.

"It makes me feel like I'm in Florida. Somehow the white towers on the water have that sense for me. All it needs is a few palm trees." Knowing that he would prefer a Victorian cottage ensconced in trees and garden, similar to Jim, I added, "We have such different tastes in living situations, don't we?"

Once Wolf's one-year contract as the interim rabbi was up, he let go of his apartment and came and went, traveling the world while still visiting me in my condo in the sky of Vancouver.

The first visit to me was after his cross-continental trip to see his two brothers. He returned from Berkeley and told me that one brother thought he shouldn't be with me. "She's not Jewish and she's just like your ex," he'd said. I didn't think I was like his ex, with the exception that we are both tall. I was very hurt but not deterred, although it caused me to feel insecure in this new relationship. How much influence did Wolf's brother have on him?

His next trip took him to Israel to work in an organization that sponsored volunteers. He loaded up medical supplies onto military trucks for the army. Here we are again — a man with a connection to the military — so many interesting juxtapositions. My man Jim left the military knowing it was not right for him to be a fighter, to be joined as brothers in arms, and here was Wolf, joined in a brother-hood of people helping to heal those in the military — another side of the coin.

I was in love with Wolf and anticipated his return. Each time he visited I was thrilled. We explored new restaurants and just enjoyed going on walks together. But I was also relieved when he left — I could be myself again.

ANOTHER FATHER FIGURE?

A few things kept popping up that disturbed the flow of this new relationship. Mainly Wolf's quiet manner. I love to talk and talk and talk, as Wolf would describe it. I was reverting back to my six-year-old self! All the while, he would be quiet. I felt judged. He confirmed this. Yes, he needed to work on his judgmental-ness — *that* was the challenge of this relationship for him. He had exhibited this trait with all the women he'd been with and was aware it was destructive to harmony. It hurt me. He had an aura of a judgmental father about him. Adding to this impression was his physical similarity to my dad — the same body build, dark eyes and hair, the Southern Mediterranean appeal that Jim had as well.

Of course, I asked myself, "In what life have I known this man before?" I again tuned in to the Spirit realm and asked for clarity about who he was to me, only to discover a strong past life connection. I was amazed as the picture of a man carrying a papyrus scroll came before my eyes. I saw the man enter a chamber to speak to my father … the pharaoh. Wolf was … the vizier … to the pharaoh. Wow! Another Egypt connection. Wolf had been a father figure to me in my lifetime in Egypt. No wonder he had that fatherly aura about him.

When I told this to Wolf, he didn't seem surprised, more intrigued, as if he was thinking, "Hmmm … maybe that *was* me." This opened up a discussion of the fact that there had been a Jewish vizier — "Don't you know the story of Joseph and the coat of many colors?"

"No, I didn't see that show." Of course, it was a biblical story, but I had long since forgotten many of my Sunday school lessons. Yet, the existence of a Jewish vizier made it seem all the more likely that a soul that chose to be Jewish in this current life also would have been a vizier under Ramses II — such a significant time period for Jews.

"There were many non-Jews who left during the flight out of Egypt," Wolf added. I began to think I must have been one of them.

Wolf knew a great deal about ancient Egypt. He knew about Akhenaten, the pharaoh who tried to turn Egypt into a monotheistic culture, and that he had disappeared mysteriously. We talked about the references to reincarnation in the Bible, particularly in the Hebrew Bible — the Old Testament in Christianity. I told him of Emperor Justinian, who had demanded that all references to reincarnation be removed from the Bible in the fifth century — a way to set himself up in a power play. I had read a few treatises by Elaine Pagels on the early church. Although I couldn't remember the details, the sentiments had stuck. The Bible had been rewritten so many times in service of whoever was in power.

The discussion of Akhenaten percolated in my mind for some time when I had a flash of realization: at the time of Ramses II, who we both agreed was the pharaoh we lived under, I had been part of an underground group who kept alive the belief in one god. For my own safety, I had to keep this mysterious identity hidden — another lifetime in which I had to suppress my voice.

This was definitely an interesting relationship, filled with new understandings and experiences.

With Jim I had tried an experiment in the spirit class in LA: we had sat opposite each other and aligned all our chakras, breathing and feeling the connection. Jim was not comfortable sitting in this position and I suspect not comfortable being so intimate. But Wolf was willing and initiated a non-sexual chakra connection as we lay together, face to face, blowing his breath into my mouth. I returned the breath, and so we continued until we drifted off to sleep. It felt like a melding of spirits. I told Wolf that we felt like angels.

INVITATION TO CONNECT

This relationship felt karmic from the start. We had so many interests in common. He chanted every morning, I meditated. Our mutual interest in the roots of religion and spirituality opened many conversations and much intellectual understanding for me. But the most impactful connection was made as I questioned when I knew him in another life. It was the key to the doorway into the mystery of my life in Egypt. It was the start of a journey to connect the reasons for all of the important lifetimes I had experienced up to that point. A profound meeting of souls.

In hindsight, the relationship was never meant to be "till death do us part," but it definitely was meant to be.

Q. With a current partner, in what areas do you feel the most connection? Does it feel like there is a higher purpose for you to be together? Does the relationship help you to connect to your soul?

If you are looking to start a new relationship, try asking yourself if you knew the person before and see what comes to you.

14

PARADISE REVISITED

What you think, you become. What you feel, you attract. What you imagine, you create.

— Buddha

WHERE TO NOW?

Even Earth Angels need a place to live. The conversation about vacation retirement locations continued. I began to seriously look for options. Wolf mentioned an upcoming conference in Panama, sponsored by *International Living* — a trip to learn about moving, retiring, or renting there. I became caught up in the sales marketing "urgency" trick to sign up for the conference. I quickly went ahead and sent in my deposit, not checking with Wolf but knowing he would certainly be interested. To my surprise, he wasn't. It took some effort to convince him to come with me. His interest was in beach communities and so was mine. I went to the seminar. Wolf sunned himself by the pool on the sixth floor of the posh Hilton in Panama City.

The bus tours west of Panama City gave a wonderful glimpse of the lifestyle I was looking for — the tropical paradise with ocean breezes, beaches, and palm trees that had been my dream since my first vision of floating down the Nile while being fanned by palm fronds.

I tried to convince Wolf to buy a condo with me. But — no success. Wolf was not interested in investing, so I went ahead on my own and put in a deposit on a condo in a tower that was not even a hole in the ground at the time. It took two years to build. During those two years, I followed Wolf back to Victoria and waited for my tropical paradise to climb into the sky. I had chosen a condo on the twentieth floor. On my first step into my new place in Panama, I was confronted with a stunning view across the bay and along the coast-line, with waves crashing against the shore far below.

It took me till the second trip there to realize, waking up one morning to the view of the swirling waves from my bedroom window, that I had actually manifested a dream I had mapped out years before. I had attempted to make this vision materialize with Jim, but his destiny took him elsewhere. But now I was with a man who had directed me straight to my dream location. Using the cues from the new man in my life and a lot of courage on my own part, I succeeded in creating my paradise on earth.

Years ago, I had an astrocartography reading by a wonderfully insightful Seattle astrologer, Ann Combs. This was something I'd never heard of before. In astrocartography, the astrologer uses a map of the entire world to chart the paths of all the planets at your time of birth. By charting these planetary paths, the map reveals the cities and regions that may influence or become important to you throughout your life. I recently pulled out the map Ann had created for me and discovered that my Pluto line runs from Toronto, where

I'd spent most of my childhood, straight south, through Panama City. Pluto represents extreme transformation. Ann told me I have plutonic energy which implies that any change I make will not be like turning a page of a book or writing a new chapter, it is more like writing a totally new book. Or … I might add, moving to a new country. The map seems prophetic now.

The Priestess Needs a Beautiful Home
With the deposit on my vacation home made, I needed to find a permanent home for myself in my home country of Canada. My year in the rental condo was nearly up. As it came closer and closer to my deadline, I still hadn't found an affordable condo that suited me. Due to new provincial regulations, a potential condo I had been waiting to come on the market slipped away, and it again was impossible to afford Vancouver. Then the discussion began with Wolf who said he loved Vancouver but wanted to go back home to Victoria.

He began looking for the perfect location in Victoria. I wanted to stay in Vancouver but I also wanted to stay with him. Wolf purchased a two-bedroom condo he was excited about — south-facing for his sun tanning.

I was excited to see it, but then my heart sank as I viewed an apartment with narrow hallways, old-lady wallpaper, and … on the ground floor.

Sitting in a little café a block away from the laundromat I had gone to as a twenty-two-year-old, I was devastatingly depressed … I began to doubt this relationship. The internet came to my rescue when I was most despondent. Back home in Vancouver, I opened my screen onto a real estate site to encounter a picture of a beautiful garden that grabbed my attention. Looking at it, this 1350-square-foot, two-bedroom, two-bath unit with an 800-square-foot terrace on the second floor above a gluten-free bakery, would have been perfect for Wolf to buy with me. I had to call him.

"Wolf, look at this place ... please! It's perfect for me."

Of course, Wolf did not look at it. This was on a Friday. On Monday I viewed it online again. I needed my friend, a property appraiser, to look at the property, and so I called her. And then I told my friend Gail about it — she then did a psychic reading for me. She said, "Lesley, you have to go and see this property yourself. Get on the ferry and go!"

Offers were being accepted until Wednesday at six. At this point it was Tuesday. OK. I arranged to meet Amanda, the property appraiser, at the condo on Wednesday morning. I got on the ferry and drove down the island highway to meet at one o'clock. Amanda and I met there with Deana, Wolf's realtor and now mine. We walked into the condo, down a long wide hallway, past the bedrooms and bathrooms and — surprise — a den. Then the condo opened into a huge living/dining space with big windows overlooking the terrace I had viewed online. I stepped through the sliding doors to a terrace with a seating area staged with dining table and chairs arranged next to a pond surrounded by pots of bamboo. Beyond that was another seating area flooded with sunlight, with a palm tree in one corner.

"This is like my garden in Vancouver — bamboo, palm tree, pond with goldfish!" And tomato plants — but of course I would not plant tomatoes. I would plant roses.

Going back in and sitting at the dining table, Amanda, Deana, and I looked at each other.

"This is my place." Amanda and the realtor agreed.

"Yes, Lesley, this is absolutely perfect for you. There is one other offer, and it is above asking." I put in a high offer. The 6 p.m. deadline rolled around; at 6:30 I got the call. "The place is yours."

"Oh my God!" The ecstasy of finding my new place in the world. Then the mad scramble to organize the mortgage, get the financing, clear out of my Vancouver condo. I had two weeks to arrange it all. Everything seemed to put up roadblocks, but I knew this was my place. I persisted. On the day of the closing, everything came together and I signed off, with Wolf backing me.

My first solo apartment. I was so excited, my mind buzzed with renovation plans. The old kitchen was the original from the 1970s, with drawers falling out and cabinets missing. The style was totally inadequate for my modern design sensibility. Maybe I would install an electric fireplace in the open concept living/dining space — a modern horizontal one with rotating colors like I'd seen in showrooms.

I couldn't believe I was returning to Victoria, but here I was, taking myself back across the water to live in my own home. And I would be close to Wolf, but not too close. Yet, all was not right in paradise.

La-La Land

Wolf's response to my design plans was "Why don't you just live with it? It's fine."

This was a side of Wolf I hadn't met before. "Well, you know I wanted an older apartment. I bought this, aside from loving the larger rooms built back then, so I could increase the value by making improvements."

It confused me that he wanted me to just live with it, accept things as they are. I wanted to make things better. To create prosperity in this place. Eventually I realized that our disagreement came down to the difference in mindset between an entrepreneur and a person who likes the security of a job.

Despite Wolf's objections, I gutted the kitchen and installed brand-new everything. Wolf, giving in, actually helped build the cabinet boxes. I installed the horizontal electric fireplace, bought wholesale in Ontario by my brother who then shipped it out to me. After adding my personal touches, I was pleased with the results. I was also pleased with an old friend's compliments. "You know, Lesley, this condo is so much more feminine, more *you*, than any home you and Jim owned together."

Although I was happy with my new home, problems persisted elsewhere. Wolf still was not sure what our relationship was, and this disturbed me. Many times he asked, "What are we?"

"We are lovers — that doesn't mean we have to live together" was always my response. I sensed he wanted a replacement for his wife and his old life. I did not fit the mold.

I took great pleasure in creating and tending my little terrace garden and was not planning to move or become anyone's wife any time soon. I'd been there, done that and now wanted to live life on my terms.

So began my re-acquaintance with the small city I had left twenty-seven years earlier. Victoria had grown up. It had become more worldly and had a new, younger vibe. New stores and restaurants were waiting to be explored. Bike paths wove through the city, past new high-rise towers — a mini version of Olympic Village on Vancouver's False Creek.

I had grown up too. My daily walk often took me past the house where I had first met Jim. "I am not the same girl I was back then." The long interlude off the island drew a strong contrast in my mind to the me of now and the me of then. My old friends knew the old me but the mask no longer fit. A well of sadness grew inside me as I realized I was no longer the girl with starry eyes who had moved to the cosmopolitan city of Vancouver twenty-seven years earlier. I still had hopes and dreams, but I did not need to create a marriage as my younger self had desired with Jim. My years in Victoria felt numbered.

Then *I* began to entertain the question of "What are we to each other?" I suggested we meet with my psychic, Ara Parisien, together. Wolf reluctantly agreed. We talked about how I am a people pleaser, and I asked Ara, "Is there a higher purpose for us being together?"

She nodded. "Yes. Wolf and you made an agreement: he would come to be with you at a certain time in your life to assist you in finding your independence, to help you be the spirit within you, a powerful woman unto yourself." Wolf, sitting next to me, seemed unmoved, but that was fine with me.

GERMANY AGAIN

During this time, I became impatient with the Jewish practice. Initially the Shabbat service was interesting, but eventually the chanting didn't assist me to raise my vibration. I was bored with the three-hour-long program. I also didn't feel connected to ceremonies that harkened back to a far-off history. I was not interested in celebrating victories and mourning failures experienced by the Jews many centuries ago that had little relevance to my life in the twenty-first century.

Our social life together had become mainly focused around Judaism. We went to the Jewish film festival to the exclusion of other non-Jewish films I wanted to see. We saw Jewish plays at the synagogue, attended musical events that were in support of Wolf's Jewish friends. All these things were interesting but not to the exclusion of the non-sectarian activities that I wanted to attend.

I know and saw how this religion is a soulful practice that guides and empowers others spiritually. The traditional rituals create stability. It was perfect for Wolf's security-loving personality. It was not perfect for me with my imaginative, creative mind. The Aquarian in me balked at being fettered by a tradition baked into a life that fit another time. I had spent many years practicing a meditation ritual that intuitively suits me. By beginning with chanting to open my chakras and then raising my mind up towards the sky, I am able to tap into the Universal Power of Spirit without any direction from the outside. I had let go of the strictures of the Anglican church when I left my family home, and I was not prepared to squeeze myself into the rigidity of a practice of rituals that didn't resonate with me.

My daily horoscopes from Co-Star often explained how I was feeling more poetically. I had downloaded this app onto my iPhone on the recommendation of my hair stylist. I enjoyed her young, ambitious energy, and we had fun comparing notes on our horoscopes. Since she had sun in Leo and I moon in Leo, we added each other to our respective apps. I later included Wolf as a friend on my app, and it often gave interesting insights into our similarities and differences. One day it read: "Talking to Wolf is like talking to a brick wall that's been standing for one hundred years. Talking to you is like talking to an ephemeral gust of whispering wind." [1] Perfect. Our minds did work so differently. My doubts about our compatibility were piling up.

---

1   Guler, Banu, Evana Bodiker, Hanna Hurr, and Stone Parkway. Co–Star. iPhone. 2020.

One ceremony at the synagogue that *did* affect me was the observance of the evening of Kristallnacht, the Night of Broken Glass. On November 9, 1938, Hitler and Goebbels urged the Nazi paramilitary forces, members of the Hitler Youth, and German citizens to attack synagogues, Jewish businesses, and Jews themselves throughout Germany and Austria. The shattering of glass windows and razing of buildings to the ground gave the day its name. Many Jews were murdered or arrested and forced into concentration camps during the wide-spread violence, and afterwards it became impossible for Jews to live safely in Germany. This event was the prelude to the expansion of the concentration camps.

I knew that there were at least a couple of people in the synagogue that evening who had direct personal experience with the camps and the horrors of that period. Others, I'm sure, knew family members or friends who had been affected.

The ceremony had a deeply visceral effect on me. As it progressed, I began to feel extremely uncomfortable and saw myself as the soldier I knew from past visions. I was horrified by the violence that I was meant to take part in and hung back, trying to make it appear I was participating even though I couldn't. I don't know if I imagined my reluctance or not, but it sufficed to ease my present-day conscience.

Still, I needed more answers. I needed to fill in the gaps in the story of Lesley and Wolf. Why was I still so afraid to be in my power?

INVITATION TO APPRECIATE

Recently my guides said to me: "The only 'sin' is non-appreciation."

In our modern world, unlike the world of Nazi Germany that kept creeping into my consciousness, we have the freedom to express ourselves as we choose and create the life path we wish to lead. The fact that we are free to speak without reprisals is a testament to the freedom of the mind that our Western culture affords us. The world's peoples are waking up to the need for personal freedom. Protests for women's rights, civil rights, the right to practice the religion of one's choice, all reflect a move towards individuality.

We should never take our freedoms for granted.

I appreciate my home where I can relax and express my creativity — just one of the many things. I appreciate the luscious yellow color of the canna flower blooming in my living room. I appreciate the subtle communication I share with my fluffy cat when she stares at me with her big green eyes. You get the picture.

Appreciation opens the heart. It is an expansion of energy outward into the future. Perhaps we can appreciate our way into a more peaceful world.

Q. Look around you. What do you appreciate? Write a list of all the things, people, places, etc. that you appreciate in your life. Don't you have much to be thankful for? Use this energy to move you.

Don't forget to appreciate yourself!

15

VEILS LIFT

By living a life based on wisdom and truth, one can discover the divinity of the soul, its union to the universe, the supreme peace and contentment which comes from satisfying the inner drive for self discovery .

— **Muata Ashby,** *Ancient Egyptian Proverbs*

DELVING DEEPER

"You had a very cushy life in Egypt, didn't you?"

"Yes. Until I had to run," I responded. I was in the midst of past life regression with a wonderful spiritual man. I had been seeking to clear up questions and details that still perplexed me about lifetimes I had already remembered, in particular the Egyptian lifetime. I was also seeking clarity about my relationship with Wolf.

As I lay relaxed on a bed, Garnet Schulhauser directed me into a light trance state.

He began by asking me how old I was and what I was wearing, which led me to a scene with an Egyptian temple off in the distance.

"Now, let's go to the place that you live. Can you describe it to me'"

"It's a squared-off building with a pool in the front. It has four pillars at the entrance. It's open air. It's kind of sand-colored, and I walk in and there's a … it's kind of an entry hall and behind is a sleeping room with a stone bed. I guess it has some kind of reed mats on it … Yeah, OK, and beyond that is another pool with columns all around it where I bathe."

"What else is there — any furniture?"

"Yes, there's a chair that has no back, just a curved seat and armrests with legs like an animal's, and pillows on the floor. It's a gathering room where people can sit and chat and eat the food that is served."

"By who?"

"Um … there's a servant who brings the food in. All the food is laid out on a round table in the middle — it's dates and breads and olives and even some green beans. You can just nibble anything you like with your fingers. It's delicious. Everything looks like it is just dripping with flavor. There's a woman rinsing dishes out in the river … a servant … So I didn't have to do the dishes! Oh, and I have a lion!"

"How did you get the lion?"

"It was given to me by my father. Oh, and I have a leopard too, but the leopard cannot reside in the house with the lion. But I can play with the leopard outside," I said, laughing.

"Are you very fond of this lion?

"Yes, I can lie down and rest my head on his mane." As I said this, I felt a deep relaxation as I leaned into the warmth of his golden mane. I was there.

"What color is the leopard?"

"A very light tan with black?"

"What do you call the leopard?"

"Hmmm … the lion is Lena. Hmmm … not a male name. It's a male lion … Cleo is the leopard. Huh … I had a cat with black spots who I named Cleo."

"Where are your mother and father?"

"They're in the court." I continued to describe my living situation: "I visit them in their rooms in the daytime. OK, here's what I see: my father, he's in a throne room. He sits at a large desk. I sit on a chair and we chat. He tells me life lessons. Oh, I'm much younger — I might be like five or six in this picture I'm seeing now."

"Then how old are you now?"

"Well, I'm around fifteen."

"So, when you first came into the scene you were around fifteen?"

"Yes." I continued, "My father is the pharaoh. He calls people in, they come in, bow down to him, hand him things to read. He asks for his food to be brought in … Oh my goodness this sounds just like Donald Trump's daughter playing on the floor in front of his desk. Yow!"

"Where is your mother? Where does she reside?"

"My mother is part of the harem. There are a lot of women in this big square sided by colonnades. Each woman has her own rooms off the common area. There's a pool in the middle. My mother lives in one of the apartments. She's not the main queen, she's just one of the harem. But I'm one of the favorite daughters … OK, that's why I get to sit and chat with my father every day. There is much business going on, so I can sit there and watch the activity, and after that I see my mother and go for walks or I play with the other children who are my siblings … Oh, yeah … there are other children of other revered women in the harem. There are servants' quarters somewhere, and their children play with us too."

"So, you go back to your own particular quarters after seeing your mother?"

"Yes, when I'm older. When I was younger I stayed with my mother."

Before this session I had already seen this scene of the women's quarters and I remembered who my mother was in that life. My Egyptian mother is my niece in this life. I feel particularly close to her. When I was trying to get pregnant, I thought she would be my child, but she was born into my brother's family. The first time I saw her, my grandmother's face flashed across her smiling baby face — still in the family!

Garnet continued. "That's interesting. Let's go back to the original scene with the temple."

"I'm around fifteen, wearing sandals, a long robe — natural linen with a bit of pale blue. I'm carrying a gold ankh. I'm wearing a lapis and gold collar and a gold chain on my hand like Indian women wear when they are getting married. Oh … actually, I have writing on my hand!" This was a revelation. "It's like henna … It's … um … the story of my life as it will unfold … telling the story of the oath that was made to present me as a bride … virgin bride."

"Has your husband been chosen for you already?"

"Yes. My father chose him …" I had already revealed to Garnet that my father was the pharaoh and that Wolf was his vizier. "I think he is a blond-haired man."

"Why do you think he has blond hair? Is he from a different country?"

"Yes, I think so. He's from Rome or somewhere else. He's very handsome — tall, muscular, dressed like a Roman soldier." I'm standing at the temple, and at this point I see him off in a distance. I recognize him as Leo. "We have not been formally introduced yet. I've just been promised to him."

"What was the purpose of that life?" Garnet asked. "What was the purpose of that incarnation? Was it just to learn about the pleasures of life?"

"No," I said. "It was to learn to moderate the pleasures of life. And to see the hardships of others, to have great feeling for the people who didn't have so much."

"And did you accomplish that?"

"Yes, because I entered the temple … as an initiate before I was married — to learn of the spirit. And to learn of the higher realms so that I knew of both the pleasures of the earthly realm and the power of the spirit. And I was meant to marry this man — I was betrothed to him. But I ate of the fruit of pleasure, of sex, and I was not acceptable anymore, so I didn't get married."

"So, who did you have sex with? Somebody else?"

"Whoa! It was Wolf's brother in this life! And he was his brother in that life too! He was a proud and stern man, very proud and autocratic."

"Did he seduce you?"

"Yes. He commanded me. And later I also had sex with my betrothed but I had to run because of indiscretions … *and* because Wolf's brother found out all my secrets. He coerced me and seduced me into talking by plying me with alcohol and fruits and perfumes. I began to trust him. He found out that I was part of an underground group that worshipped only one god and that we were against the priest. We did not believe the priest was the one to give commands.

155

We knew that it was God who commanded us."

I couldn't believe it — Wolf's brother was the one who betrayed me! This was a revelation, that the two had been brothers before, both powerful, judgmental men. It also explained the closeness between them in our present lives and perhaps why his brother took an immediate dislike to me.

God, I was so naïve with Wolf at the beginning — out of my depth with him and his family. I was so "white bread" in my anxiety to please, to be perfect. I was guileless in the face of men with such judgmental and manipulative personalities.

So yes, my life in Egypt was a cushy life. It was a beautiful life. That is, until I was betrayed. Until I had to run. Politics had a hand in the disruption of my perfect life just as it had caused the dissolution of the life of Akhenaten, the first pharaoh to believe in one god.

Now I knew why I had to run! But, what happened beyond the steps of the temple was yet to be revealed to me.

A HIGHLAND FLING

Next, I was treated to a life I'd never seen before.

Continuing the session, Garnet suggested: "Let's move into a scene of an important day in a lifetime that's pertinent right now — a day you consider important because there is something happening. What do you see around you?"

"Well, it seems like I'm going to another century, another country. I'm seeing a wedding day. It's May Day, where everybody's wearing flower garlands. It must be Scotland because I'm wearing a kilt and a white blouse of eyelet cotton. It may be the Middle Ages. It's very colorful, so bright and almost pastel. Everything's just youthful and like spring. I don't think I'm getting married ... No — I'm part of a celebration of a marriage. I'm part of the ceremony."

"What color is your kilt?"

"I want to say pink but that can't be." I laughed. "Maybe red and white with a little black, some orange in it. It's quite a light color. Seems like the young people have lighter tartans. It's gay. The atmosphere is gaiety. We're celebrating the marriage of ... my older sister. I'm a child. I'm ... I don't know .... maybe nine. The bride and groom are standing in front of an archway of flowers and ribbons. The bride is wearing white lace and a long tartan skirt, the groom wears a kilt with a sporran and a black jacket with braiding, shoes with buckles on the front. He's very handsome. I'm very happy for my sister. There's a big feast at a long table. People are dancing. It must be medieval because everybody is eating with their hands — pagan — a bacchanalia. And they're drinking mead and some have wine skins."

"Are you old enough to drink the mead?

"I'm not supposed to but I sneak some — bad girl! There's music: a bagpipe, a pipe band, and some fiddles. It's lively dancing music, you know, Scottish dancing — swinging and all the ribbons are flowing in the air. I just see the ribbons! There's a boy that I like ... He's a little older, about fourteen. He likes me, got his eye on me. I'm kind of flirtatious.

"Oh, I just realized this is Wolf ... Ahhh ... He kisses me and we take a walk. He gets me on the ground and then presses me to have sex. I resist and start beating him on his back and push him off. He gets off me. I don't scream or tell anyone ... I didn't want to get caught. For one thing, I've had a little bit of mead, and for another, I have been very flirtatious with him. I just skip back to the celebration as if nothing has happened. I was kind of happy that I got him interested but was able to fend him off ... What a cheeky little girl! He came back later. The fact is, I think he was a little embarrassed and apologized. He said he got carried away because he liked me so much."

"Did you continue to see each other after that?"

"I was too young for him, but he flirted with me in the cobblestone streets. We walked and talked together as he came back from lessons. He was a good friend and looked out for me."

The feeling of gaiety that permeated this memory lingered until Garnet asked if Wolf had married me.

I answered, "No. He married someone else. I was quite flirtatious, quite sexual. Oh! … I was reviled by the townspeople … I had turned to prostitution to support myself, and the man with money who intended to marry me heard the town gossip and turned his back on me too. I was beaten down and died in the street. The lovely, fun girl had been taken advantage of by powerful heartless men. Life was hard in the Middle Ages."

Then another shocking memory was reignited. "After this life, I chose the life as the nun." But my soul's choice for repentance didn't really pan out, as I had discovered years earlier upon meeting Jonas.

MUSICAL INTERLUDE

Before beginning the session, Garnet and I had discussed what I wanted to get out of the regression. I was most interested in filling in the gaps in my Egyptian lifetime. I got that and more!

When I told him I would be writing a book about past lives, he asked me if I had any writers working with me from the other side. He explained that, while writing his own books, he had help from spirit. Before the session, I didn't. So, near the end of the regression he asked if I saw anyone to help me write.

"Wilson Pickett." Although it was my own instinctual answer, it still confused me. "How could a musician help me write?" I said, asking and then answering my own question. "Well, he wrote songs." Then the meaning dawned on me. "Aha! Songs are not written completely in the same tone. There are parts that tell a story. Then there is a chorus. Different rhythms, cadence, instrumentals contribute to create a more interesting piece. So it is OK — in fact, a good idea — to incorporate different voices, prose, and poetry in one book." Knowing I was receiving help from the spirit world gave me the courage to trust that my own voice would be guided. Writing a book, I could follow my intuition as I do in my daily life. And so I began.

I had also asked Garnet to ask me in trance state if I would stay with Wolf.

My answer for myself was, "Not for long."

Invitation to Participate

While I have had great recall of other lifetimes on my own, I have also achieved profound awareness about past lives when led by someone else.

All I can add to this chapter is to consider doing a past life regression with an experienced regressionist.

In the future, I will be giving presentations about past lives and will be leading group regressions. If interested, please check out my website and leave an email address to receive notifications about upcoming events.

16

RISE OF THE DIVINE FEMALE

Taking joy in living is a woman's best cosmetic.
— Rosalind Russell

PONDERING SCOTLAND

The memory of dying as a prostitute did not upset me. I considered the time in which it had occurred and realized that it was a period when girls and women had no power. I had been taken advantage of by men who wanted to own the gaiety I emanated. My love of life had been stolen by thieves, men with black hearts and anger at their lots in life.

The patriarchy of the past is now being challenged by women unwilling to be shut down and subjugated. I am one of them. The lessons of my past lives drive me onward. It is our time now.

During the past life regression, Garnet guided me to close out that vision of my life and death in Scotland with an affirmation — what I could take away as a gift to myself.

I said: "I will remember the gaiety of the wedding, the multitude of ribbons floating in the air, and the joy I felt in being alive in that moment."

Perhaps seeing this lifetime was a healing of the serious and obedient nine-year-old girl who had been silenced while trying to voice her opinions during a family lunch.

I deliriously devalued my femaleness early on in this life. The anxiety I felt in my body — trying to be perfect, trying to fit in as my family frequently moved to new homes across the country where I had to make new friends — caused me to live in my imagination as a young girl. As a teenager, I was always under the watchful eye of my mother. Demands such as "don't swing your hips so much as you walk" made me tighten up in defence and prevented me from really enjoying living in my body.

To experience my Egypt lifetime in such a visceral way was healing. I felt loved — I experienced all the pleasures of life that were afforded me. I loved my life and I loved myself. As I revisited my Egypt life in my current lifetime, I began to absorb this consciousness. During the lockdown period of the Covid-19 pandemic, I swanned around my condo in flowing robes, integrating the princess/priestess into my earthly life. I was living the joy of being female.

OH SO FEM

As I sat to meditate one morning, the words of the song "Beyond the Horizon" by Bob Dylan went through my mind. I knew it was a message from Jim. That he was over the horizon, waiting for me. Or … was I the one waiting for him to come through? My heart took me on a trip through my playlist, looking for the song. "Take This Waltz" by Leonard Cohen then struck a chord about love on the deepest level.

I'm reminded of the question that I had put to my friend Shelley as I was beginning to see Wolf: "Why would he want *me*?" He seemed so erudite, I didn't feel I was his intellectual equal like his ex-wife. And I didn't have the kind of power in the world that she had.

"Am I hearing myself say that now?!" What about all the people I had orchestrated to transform hotel ballrooms into magical forests for guests to feast in amidst evergreen trees, under a canopy of twinkling stars? What about all the props, the trucks, the timing, the love of drama that I had summoned to bring these things to fruition? Was it in vain? No. It was a luxury I afforded many people to live, enjoy, converse about, and feel connected with. What a gift I gave of my creativity and my organizational skills!

I had to remind myself that I was and am a powerful woman. I am learning to value myself on my own terms. I dive deeper.

Leonard Cohen's music speaks of love for women on a much deeper level … of essence. I know now that I am the female essence that Wolf saw and felt, was attracted to and compelled by. What more could a man want?

Star Light, Star Bright

Recently while reading Ariel Tomioka's book *On the Breath of the Gods*, the sentence "The monster in your dreams can be your own power chasing you" popped from the page. [1]

"Hmmm … What is my monster?"

"Fear of expressing myself, voicing my truth" — not a surprise.

---

1   Tomioka, Ariel. *On the Breath of the Gods*. Helios House, 1990.

This answer was then followed by a memory of a guided meditation in a workshop I had attended.

A suggestion from the leader: "So, I want you to visualize a power animal to join you on the journey you'll be going on. You'll be going to a market hall, and I want you to leave your monster behind at the door before you enter."

My vision opens to a magnificent white horse. As I cross the draw-bridge seated proudly on my white steed, I leave behind the stifled feeling that comes from being told what to eat, what to wear, how to behave. My blue blouse becomes a flowing white gown. I enter a beautiful banquet hall with rich, enchanting murals decorating the ceiling. People are clapping for me. Then, the ceiling opens up to the stars. A star comes down and touches me, and I know who I am.

As I leave the hall, a regal Pegasus swoops down before me. I settle onto its back, and it flies me into the star-studded sky.

"Oh, how amazing!" I thought to myself as I opened my eyes.

This reminded me of the dream I had awoken from the night before. In the semi-dream state, I felt in my essence, in my spirit, that I was the scent of my favorite perfume. As I was remembering these experiences, my guides told me, "Now, it is time to live in that essence while you are awake and going about your daily life. It is very female and powerful in that female essence."

As if to confirm this, my writer guides wrote me a poem.

PINK

Persephone, perseverance, pearls, purpose, pupil

Pages turn to reveal the lotus blossom's secret scent

That floats out into the atmosphere requiring healing

RISE OF THE DIVINE FEMALE

The wavelengths of the mental energy

Of the many require a new spoken word

A new expression of love

That obliterates the old understanding

Of loving patience and perseverance

Love blows through the seams, through the seeds,

Through the autumn leaves,

Through the power of persuasion

Forward motion makes its advent

And the string of pearls

Drip from the neck of all who see the vision

Of the lotus blossom opening its petals

And releasing its scent

Into the atmosphere of love

Pitching the pink.

All pink is not the same

Many pinks are of power

Other pinks are of powder

Of performance lasting in a poof

Some pinks perform perception

Of the likes of which

One does not usually perceive

But pink is definitely the color of love

Regardless of its expression

Pink can be soft and sweet

GEMS OF TIME

Pink can be harsh and vibrating with rage

Pink can be outré when paired with black

Pink can be kink in the hair

Or perception of care

Pink can arrive on a cloud of blue

Pink can be for you

Or fur of poodles

Pink is also your purpose

Pink can lead towards purple

Pink can bring in the new

Pink can be old and powerful

And wear old gold as well

Pink is the powder of love

The blush that's on the face

That which holds the whole together

In an understanding

Of what is fake and what is pure.

Let us take a look at the power pink

It is a medium purple-pink

That brings forth love and perception

It is not powder-puff pink

It is purpose pink

Purple and purpose perform miracles

Miracles like the scent of the lotus

Floating into the atmosphere

Catching other molecules of purple-pink

And floating as in a balloon of iridescence

To burst upon the mind of those who seek

The peace of mind the scent brings

Peace be still

Peace be powerful

Peace be pinkish

Peace be me and peace be you

Purposeful purplish pink is proud

Peace

Let pink bring you pride in your purpose

Pinkish purple-pink

Proud pink

Proud of one's purpose

Pride in the purposeful actions

Of the powerful inner knowing

Pride in the pride of lionesses

Pride in the power of loving kindnesses

Giving purpose to the pleasant days of life.

AUTHOR ...

The day after this encouraging poem spilled down to me from the Universe, I sat to meditate and my guides instructed: "You don't need any cards today."

"I'll just pull one card. If I get the Ace of Swords, that's a good sign." I began to shuffle the cards, and one fell out onto my lap. I turned it over. The Ace of Swords! "That's just a little chilling!" I said out loud to myself. I was told yesterday that this card represents T. S. Eliot. I thought, "I hope this is who writes the poems with me."

"OK, who else is with me today?"

"Jonas and Jim."

And continuing on ...

Persephone, purpose, perfect, pure pink.

Guides again instructed: "Your Sì perfume is the earth scent. Your Pivoine Suzhou perfume is the Aquarian heart/mind scent that drifts as the mystic magic of the moon.

"You must wear this perfume today when you go outside so that you are in a cloud of magic rather than a cloud of smoke and ash. You have transcended the holy war and have opened to the Age of Aquarius. The priestly being that is you is of beautiful scent."

I have long associated the souls of deceased loved ones with a scent. My grandmother walked past me as I inhaled the lily of the valley in my garden. My aunt, my dad's sister, joined me and my dad one day as we chatted, her presence a distinctive musky scent that she had worn while she was alive.

ANOTHER PINK DAY

As I began today, the little juncos came to feed on the seeds of the devolving grasses. A hummingbird greeted me at the window, hovering for a few seconds to say hello before finding little to feed on in my garden and soaring away to more fertile banquets.

Jonas joined me as I settled into a meditation. "Now, there is a reason for your purple-pink crystal on your altar, for you will indeed be bringing in your understanding of feminine power today. The work has already been done around the history of women. Generations of female scholars and artists have accomplished this through story-telling, writing books, and creating other forms of art.

"Your understanding is on a different level. Your purpose is to help women to open to their own will center — the solar plexus — and to encase it in a very, very rigid silver band that maintains its integrity for the golden life that each girl, each woman desires for herself. There are many who are still working to find their own voice in the world, those who do not realize that their own voice is already within them. They are still looking outside of themselves to find their way. Integrity comes from 'in.' *In*tegrity implies the power from within — the strength that brings forth the personal power of purpose with the pink power in the world."

I have not always felt strong in my feminine power, and the poem from my guides expresses that I have built it up within me. But I did consider this years ago on my trip to California with Jim. I was given a message by another spiritual woman that shocked me and got me pondering about the male/female dichotomy.

"You are female, Lesley. You are acting like a male," Cheryl said. And to Jim, she said, "You are behaving like a female." These statements perturbed me for some time. While I did like Cheryl's idea that females only need to work for four hours a day due to their use of intuitive abilities, I still like to be in charge. I have always been good at organizing, setting goals, and accomplishing things. I came to the conclusion that while Cheryl's ideas for categorizing male and female behavior worked for her, they did not work for me.

Jonas recently lectured me about becoming too isolated. "You realize that in this world today one must bring out the masculine power and play within it for periods of time. The masculine power is what brings the feminine power into the world and expands its beauty, not just in the physical sense, for the world to see. For this dynamic to occur — taking you from a very feminine period of concentration and then bringing out the masculine — is a challenge for you. It requires great heart, great courage, a love of the self's purpose, and a complete alignment with this purpose and the power that is within."

After much life experience, reflection, and insight from my guides and my past lives, I understand that I play in both male and female energy. I am aware that my male energy is what takes me out into the world, and that my female energy is about feelings, intuition, and inner visions, all the aspects that I use to create and guide my life. Both are necessary in equal measure.

GENERATIONS OF PINK

There are innumerable powerful women to emulate in the world today. For me, one of them is Hillary Clinton, who works hard for the human rights of women.

My intuitive power was activated one day in 2017 as I watched a newscast about Clinton's loss during the US federal election of the previous year. Although the election results were old news by now, there was still much talk about why she had not won. As I watched the discussion, the words of the song "Go Where You Wanna Go" floated through my mind.

"This should be interesting," I thought. What followed, from out in the universe, was a story of female power lived large. I have no facts to back it up, but it was intriguing.

Again, "Go where you wanna go …" The lyrics kept running through my head …

"Oh, Mama Cass …"

"Yes. You got it," my guides chimed in.

"OK … And …?"

"She's come back, blasting onto the scene as Ariana Grande. She is the reincarnation of Mama Cass."

"Wow! That gives me chills all down my legs! I just watched a newscast about the bombing at the Manchester Arena where Ariana Grande had given a concert. Twenty-two people, including young girls and their mothers, were killed by an Islamic terrorist, presumably hating the message of power that the singer was imparting to girls."

"Yes, you get the connection. Mama Cass created beautiful songs that expressed a woman's voice."

My guides had dropped in for a visit and let me in on Mama Cass's past lives. True or not, I can't say. But here goes …

"Her obsession with food began in earlier lifetimes. She had died of starvation during the Holocaust, and not coincidentally she chose to be born Jewish again in this lifetime. She had died several times of starvation. She has come back as Ariana Grande to show young girls the way to their personal power. As you know, it is a woman's world now."

I'm not sure how true this story is, but this attack was another sign that the girls *are* rising up, that their voices are a powerful threat to the status quo.

"It is the new young generation of girls who will take over world control, world power. They will lead the world into peaceful accommodation of success for women and help obscure the lines of differences between people," the guides added.

The timing of the bombing in Manchester, coming several months after the US election, seemed to juxtapose the issues around female power — one young woman influencing girls everywhere, one older woman trying to break through the glass ceiling of politics. The world was witnessing generations of women and girls — baby boomers, Gen Xers, millennials, and Gen Zers — all working to make change.

"But Hillary lost," I reminded the guides.

My guides had something to say about this. "If Hillary had won, she would not have been able to execute her plans. She would have been blocked at every turn by the patriarchy in Washington. It was not yet time for a woman to be in that office." Then they added, "Hillary was not feminine enough to be accepted by the patriarchal government — sad to say. Her power was threatening to men. But … by losing the election she has activated women the world over, and that is a far greater service to humanity."

"I guess the country first has to taste the opposite of female power in a man who uses women as playthings and pawns for his own power," I added sarcastically.

Hillary Clinton's run for presidency had been the hope for women everywhere. But she was defeated by an angry, misogynistic man who lied and manipulated his way into the presidency. The grieving was palpable in the atmosphere for months after the election. Then the grief turned to divine anger and action as Trump's inauguration precipitated the Women's Marches in cities and towns all over the world. The 1960s' rallying cry of "Power to the People" has transformed into "Power to Women." A new generation of protest has been born.

Trumpism stirred the emotions of the country, of North America, of the world for five long years and still is as of this writing. Men brandishing swords and torches, women irate, rage bubbling up inside, indignation reigning in the zeitgeist at the diatribes spewed out on social media by one man. It is our responsibility to carry the protest

against Trumpism and the patriarchy into the future, to keep channeling the energy of the Women's March as we fight for a better world.

Shortly after the election, I channeled a letter to Hillary regarding
the good she was doing in the world. I was meant to send it. But, alas,
the "who am I to do this?" reared its head once again.

I only really disappointed myself with this failing. My guides
continued to encourage me by guiding me on a deep meditation one
day as I sat in my red swivel chair at my meditation desk ......

Invitation to Visualize Your Power

Visualization is a powerful tool. It engages positive
emotions that enhance any affirmations you are using to
manifest your life dreams.

While in the deep meditation below, I was led into this
visualization. Everything is geared for my likes. You can
rewrite the details of this meditation to suit you — make
it reflect the things you love.

Listen. Feel your female power. Be in your Magnificence.

Or write your own affirmations and listen to your own
voice.

Swan Throne Meditation

Turn the key to the vault. Open the door. Walk into the
white temple. Take the steps down the stairs of white
marble into a deep iridescent blue. Open your eyes to
the sparkle in the room. Glints of gold sparkle like fire-

flies, and there is a gold throne with the wings of a swan and the eye of Horus. Be seated in this gold chair. Turn it around and see a flaming purple flower rising, rising, rising to a white figure on a white throne. You are the figure. You have your white poodle next to you, and you have your white leopard next to you. At your feet is a white tiger with its warm body for you to rest your feet upon. All these animals love you and hold you accountable to present the beautiful purple flower that rises up into the sky. You present this as a gift to all the gods that the one God has distilled from all of the potential interests of humanity. You are represented by the Magus for all things within the Magnus — creativity, beauty, writing, money, power, healing, and arts. Magnificent powers of transformation are yours. You are a creator of magnificent proportions. You have been like a muzzled bear. Take off the muzzle. Your fur is now white. You can wear any color of animal skin that you choose. Ermine. Hold yourself in high contempt if you do not continue writing. Hold yourself in higher regard in your magnificence of expression. The writing is an expression of you, and you are an expression of spirit.

BE IN YOUR MAGNIFICENCE!

17

WOLF WAS A CHARM

We must be willing to let go of the life we've planned so as to have the life that is waiting for us.

— Joseph Campbell

PRIESTESS

The priestess that I had incorporated into my psyche began to resurface and inform me about my leaving Egypt with the Jews. I saw a vision of myself living with the people I had escaped with as they searched for a homeland outside of Egypt. I "married" a Jewish man and took on the household roles required of women in that ancient world. But it didn't take long for me to become dissatisfied with the menial tasks, having been highly educated in the spiritual arts and ways of the world in the privileged life I had left. I came to view the people around me with a jaundiced eye. They seemed like sheep to me — powerless without the guidance of a male leader. Did not my upbringing emphasize meditation and connection to the power of the cosmos? I left these people to sneak back into Egypt, to live incognito in my beautiful empire.

This was the final lesson about Egypt that was activated while being with Wolf. These visions seemed to surface in tandem with my disillusionment with the modern Jewish faith, and together they began to erode my feelings for Wolf.

Jonas contributed to my doubts with a message one morning: "It has been seven years since Jim's passing. Over those seven years, you have been given a great gift of learning how to be on your own and find your own inner power through both male and female aspects. You have built up your inner confidence. You are releasing yourself from the need for a man to fulfill your male aspects and to propel you forward."

"Love Is a Many-Splendored Thing …"

The song by Sammy Fain and Paul Francis Webster sprang from my lips as I got up from my desk. I had been writing about feeling lonely and wondering if I should stay with or leave Wolf. Many times over the past few years with Wolf, as I sat to meditate, this song would filter through my mind. It is a sad song — the theme song from the movie of the same name with William Holden, where he has a love affair with a beautiful Chinese doctor. Despite loving each other, they have to separate because their cultures are so different. The song always brought up doubts that my relationship with Wolf could work. It was, of course, a reference to the gulf between our world views and lifestyles that was created by his Jewish faith and traditions and my Aquarian, futuristic focus. Sadly, I agreed with the song and the movie's ending.

Jonas again spoke: "Think of your relationship as a charm — an additional magic charm to your life force on your path. You fulfilled the last charm by inviting Wolf to visit you in your place in Panama.

While there you realized you two would not be leading a life in Panama together as you had imagined, and he realized that was not the life for him.

"You will be relieved to know that Wolf will find someone new who can be his muse as you were. You were a powerful force to assist him to open his heart again after his divorce, and for some time he was happy to satisfy your needs. But, it became necessary for him to re-establish his own needs as priorities, which led him to engage more deeply with his faith and community.

"You know he said several times that he arrived at the same place with you in three years as he did in forty years with his wife. He is well aware that he has something that involves his own soul development in his future which doesn't include you."

Where Is This Going?

The day of the breakup saw turmoil in my heart. A conversation about our relationship seemed to bring me deeper and deeper into pain and confusion. It did not end well. He told me, "You should leave now."

I got up off the sofa and left.

As I walked towards my own apartment, a wave of bitterness, a new feeling for me, took over. The acrimonious breakup got me thinking spiteful thoughts. "So now that I no longer have him in my life, I'll move to Toronto as I had been contemplating. I don't need him to run my life." Then I spent several months debating, "Is this the right thing to do?"

Sitting to meditate one day, I pulled the Nine of Wands from my Thoth deck. The question was, "Is this the right move for me?" The card indicated "you will experience your energy going far beyond the boundaries you thought existed." [1]

Jonas jumped in with an answer of his own: "Toronto is strength. The difference between Victoria and Toronto is palpable to you. The energy of this beautiful island is lackadaisical and dreamy and hopeful, but not determined.

"The energy of Ontario, Toronto specifically, is one of determination. You will find your niche there, which you did not find in Victoria this time round. Your place is by the lakeshore. Somewhere along Lake Ontario you will find the energy that you can afford — the view of Toronto in your side window will give you a glimpse of the office tower in which your father worked when you were a little girl."

I thought about my nieces and nephew in the East. The guides told me: "You do not need to be cute, chatty, or perky like the young women in your family who live in Ontario. You need to be the strong, calm, dare we say silent creator of energy around them, infusing the room with power and sparkling light to create a realm of influence through the younger people."

Next, Jonas gave me a lesson on the building of the characteristics of the City of Toronto.

"You have energetic connections in Toronto — the strength of the Brits and the strength of the Germans. Your family tree is revealing of great strength and determination through the Scottish, Welsh, English, and Germanic strains of DNA." My direct family is Scottish, Welsh and English. My sister-in-law's family is German.

"Determination — the Germans brought their determination to Canada, as did the Scottish and English. The City of Toronto was and

---

1 Ziegler, Gerd. *Tarot: Mirror of the Soul: Handbook for the Aleister Crowley Tarot.* Weiser Books, 1998. 114.

is built by people of determination."

I felt chills down my spine when Jonas told me this.

"Building and burgeoning forth — all the cultures that are drawn to Toronto have contributed to this powerhouse of energy. It is the engine that drives Canada forward and produces powerhouses of people. The young who have left Toronto to seed other cities take with them the drive to progress. They allow for the burgeoning forth of new ideas in new cultural hotspots."

My niece and her boyfriend were about to move to Vancouver. We seemed to be switching places. Jonas agreed: "So you see Toronto has moved to Vancouver. Millennials are like the bees who need to fly off and create a new hive when the one they are living in has become too large. They are being sent out — flung into the world, flowering in other areas and expanding their own natures as well through cultures in different locales."

I continued to have ambitions to accomplish things just like when I was drawn to Vancouver after sixteen years in Victoria. I felt pulled to the big city that suited my energy at the time. That move had been for Jim's development as much as mine. But now, it was solely my time, and I needed to follow this inclination to move again.

Designing a New Condo

During this period of intense channeling, I was given instructions for the fulfillment of my dreams.

As I lay in bed at night, I would dream of moving to Toronto. Visions of a beautiful condo trickled through my imagination. The layout came first — a kitchen with windows on two sides that reached down to the counters and afforded a magnificent view of Lake Ontario. This was not like anything that was being built, but …

it's *my* vision! I'd paint the bedroom a deep blue like the night sky, and it would also have a full-length window onto a balcony that overlooked the lake. It would be filled with white furnishings, all new.

Going home one evening at sunset, tears rolled down my face as I drove past the new high-rises being built in downtown Victoria. The scene reminded me of my dreams — but in which city were these dreams meant to manifest?

I booked an appointment with my psychic friend to confer with her regarding a move to ...? I told Ara, who lives in a cottage nestled in the trees, "I want to live in the sky again." While I loved my condo on the second floor with the terrace garden that enclosed me in a magical world of my own, I began to want to have a sky view.

I told her, "I think it should be in Toronto — although maybe it should be in Victoria."

She paused for a moment, and as she tuned in, she said, "Yes, I think it's Toronto."

She encouraged me to visualize where I would live. Of course, my subconscious was already working on it. She said to do this every night before I went to sleep — already doing this — and feel myself really being there. My imagination began to furnish the living room with two white, no, mauve sofas, two stools with tiger-print velvet sitting in front of the fireplace. Would these colors go together ...? These visualizations propelled me forward to make the move. Though I don't *yet* live in that large condo, I do have a lake view and a wraparound balcony from which to view it.

My friend Bernadette, who had initiated my spiritual journey many years earlier, told me that I will always have a home. In a card reading she did for me, she saw that this guarantee was a result of things I had done in my past lives and she left it at that.

THE BELL RINGS

The next day, the collective group of spirits The Bells chimed in and spoke to a deeper reason for a move. "Lesley, you are the one chosen to speak for us in the English language. Most other Bells on Earth are forming words in different languages. All words spoken are given in love. We send you flowers as symbols of our love."

A POEM FROM THE BELLS

The waves crash on the shore
And brush the sands of time
Perpetuate the life
That the sands hold within
Each grain of sand is like a universe
Enabling the viewer to see
The potential within themselves
For envisioning a future
Built on wisdom from the past.

The channeling that came from The Bells while I meditated required me to raise my vibration to a much higher level than in the past. Receiving from them was often a visual experience, and sometimes I struggled with the wording of the messages they intended. It all depended on the clarity of my mind.

The Bells continued with instructions: "Do not pounce on any particular vision. Just take the step towards the first vision in your mind. As you move forward, all manner of things —streaks of electricity, streaks of vision, streaks of eons — will pass by and through you as you pass your days on the earth plane.

"You have become invisible to many, for they cannot grasp your visions. The bounds of the earth plane have held sway on you long enough for you to experience the power of spirit through engagement in the environment in which you live. But you now seek to find the environment that flows with your visions. And that is the journey you are embarking upon.

"The breadth and depth of this vision will be revealed for others to see as you outline your approach through your writing. That is the purpose of this book — to assist others in going home to the power of spirit incarnate. The Earth does not need to be a boundary to spirit. The Earth is a poetic expression of spirit in many models, in many forms, in many activities.

"Even those who allow themselves to be caught in the web of self-destruction can be assisted out of the miasma and can lean towards the light of love. All beings on Earth at this time have come for the purpose of training themselves into the light of love.

"Perpetual motion requires that you change locations as soon as is feasible to make the love experience adequate to your health, mental and emotional. We do not want this transition to be a momentous burden or a stress-creating event in your life, and therefore we give you daily guidance on your situation and what is to be done moving towards this new path you will embark upon in a new location.

"If you choose to move to Ontario, as you have, all will be put into place and you will be guided every day in ways that will draw you in that direction. Your home will be your castle once again but in a new location."

Invitation to Your Personal Power

To make such a big move, I knew I needed to pull together strength from all my resources. I developed a third chakra mantra to repeat to myself to help me gather my powers.

The third chakra is the will center. It signifies the power to draw strength into your center to combine Earth Power and Spirit Power in the alchemical process of transmuting beingness into action for the world's transformation.

Q. Do you ever doubt your capability to make certain changes in your life? Recognize that assistance is all around you. Use this mantra as an affirmation to boost your confidence while breathing into your solar plexus.

Third Chakra Mantra

"The energy of the sun within me gives me the strength and power to create the beautiful life that I desire. I hold myself capable of …

[fill in your own words].

I relax into the power within."

18

THE INEVITABLE

My life is better with every year of living it.
— Rachel Maddow

You Say It's Your Birthday

My girlfriend and I sat outside a café in 36°F weather, wearing our masks until the cappuccinos were brought out — the only option for celebrating my midwinter birthday during the pandemic.

"Did you receive anything from Wolf?" asked my friend Lesley.

"It really hadn't occurred to me, but no. Who knows? Maybe he'll send me a card. He always sent one to his ex."

The conversation continued on about my plans to move. "You know," I said, "I had a dream last night about moving and putting my condo up for rent instead of selling. Now I'm undecided … I think I'll just let it lie for a while. It'll probably be answered for me."

I headed home and opened the mailbox. There was the card from Wolf. It gave me a warm feeling all over. "At least he still cares."

On the front of the card were pansies, just like the little faces I had planted that welcomed me to the kiss of spring in the air. I adored them as I stepped out onto my deck each day. "How did he know? Sweet."

I opened the card to a handwritten poem entitled "Amazing," more bitter than sweet. It stabbed my heart, penetrated my mind with doubts, and permeated my entire body with a feeling of unease I had trouble shaking off.

A folded page fell out of the card. It was a bank notice declaring the end of August of that year as the termination date of my mortgage, which I shared with Wolf. "Well that really does answer the question!" I said to myself. The card held two answers — the completion of the relationship and the completion of my sojourn in Victoria.

"It is settled. So why is my heart not settled?"

The answer came to me the next day in the form of a poem as I closed my eyes to meditate.

AMAZING

Amazing
I will never be able to use that word again
After you used it as the header and footer
To the bitterness of the poem of love
Sent to me on my birthday
So much water under the bridge
So much sand in the eye
So much prayerful crying
To understand the true nature
Of this love affair

THE INEVITABLE

Tomorrow is a new day
For that matter today is a new day
Amazing.

Hopes and dreams fulfill
In an instant
In the blink of an eye
Focus in the present
And feel the unctuous
Perpetual love spilling into the pool of teardrops
Meant to hold the power of eternity
Punishment of the self is not the answer
Punitive actions only cut away
That which was gained
In the blink of the eye
In the honing in
On the powerful purpose
For the soul wants what it wants
The heart just goes along for the ride.

Hearts and hugs for tomorrow
Of course it's Valentine's Day
The homeless hope for melting of the snow
You hope for honing in on the home of the soul
With footsteps step by step
Making amends to no one
And holding yourself in the heartfelt harmony
With the purpose at hand.

The purpose of the soul
Prioritizes the many days ahead
And purports to be alert
To the powers in the world
That direct that purpose
Plowing under the past
Is the only pathway forward
Plowing the path ahead
For the ease of passage
Is the perpetual desire
For satisfaction of the soul.

I finished the poem. Sat back. The energy was magical. "Well, that was fun," I said out loud. "Words fleeting, flit by like the butterfly, and make me sit. quick. jiminy cricket. pine for wisdom. poke through the veil to fly to the stars." I love it when words float through my mind. These were words that Wolf rued. He had wanted me to play with *him*, not with my own creativity.

"Your name will be mud if you do not do this book, if you do not finish it." I heard these words regularly. They were both admonishment and encouragement from the guides.

"The purpose of your time here in Victoria is coming to an end. You're wrapping it up just as you're wrapping the package that Wolf has given you — the package for the star who needs to shoot her arrows elsewhere. Love comes in many packages. Love fills the soul and works its magic. You cannot be the woman you chose to be without allowing the magic to penetrate and perpetuate your life.

"We like the 'P.' It is a letter that pushes (publishes) outward into the world," they said, explaining why they use certain words and sounds to emphasize a point.

"You struggle with leaving Wolf. We suggested that you do a prayer for him every night. Do this. Write a prayer for him. Put it on paper. It is more of an affirmation of love for the dear man."

"Oh god, why am I so pained at leaving him?"

Guides replied: "It is not guilt you feel. It is the pain of letting go of a love. Guilt is just the top note. He needs to find his heart again. He saw it in you."

So, I wrote: "I hold the feeling in my heart for you still as I feel propelled towards a different future than Victoria or what our relationship held for me, and that is the crux of the matter.

"I have no criticism of you. The irritations that you speak of are irritations of the earthly moment. I hold you in my heart as a powerful man. You are a soul with great power. You have assisted me, inspired me, ignited me on my path. I do see your beautiful practice of prayer and devotion to God as your discipline." Perhaps if I had said these things to Wolf before … But it is too late now. I am moving on …

As I wrote, I thought, "These stories of the past that I am writing feel like episodes in a TV show because the girl in them is not me anymore … I am leaving the past versions of myself behind. Does everyone get to this point in their lives? Does everyone feel this way when they're older?"

All of my guides spoke to me then: "No, our darling, it is a wrapping up. Not everyone has this experience. You are ready to take on the persona of your soul full time — walking in the world as a fulfilled woman, as a create-ure of the magnificence of God planted on the earth plane. Each being, each human, is this. You are just becoming acutely aware of it — no longer plodding, no longer making amends to anyone. The powers that be on Earth do not run things for you anymore. The powers that be, that are alert to your needs, are those in Spirit, with great wealth of understanding, of heart, of fulfillment. You know female power is on the rise in the world."

THE GOLD BALL

Around the time I was contemplating a move to Toronto to cries of friends — "But Victoria is so beautiful! Why would you want to do that?" — I was given instructions from my guides to imagine a gold ball in my left hand and a silver one in my right. These were meant to replace the finger mudras in traditional meditation: gold for the metaphysical world, silver for the outer world. Then a channeling came through ... "You are settling into a deep sleep, crackling fires, the little embers floating out into the deep blue sky and up into the holographic universe, spiraling, spiraling, spiraling into the muse's most dynamic energy. We are allowing you into this new world in a new way today. You are granted entrance. Your book will be written with beauty and guidance in mind. The powers that be are working with you strongly" — a phrase that I hear often when any doubt creeps into my mind. "It is the heart that needs to be opened more, not the mind. Your mind is prepared for anything. Your heart works overtime to prevent you from being hurt. You can calm down, you can wear the beautiful white clothing. We guide you every day. Every day is a new day. You know that your word is as good as gold.

"You are pitching the gold ball out into the world over the stone fence. You see Victoria as a stone fence of old."

The metaphor was not lost on me. Coming back out of the channeling, I remembered a favorite fairy tale that my dad read to me as a child. In the story, two children were playing next to a stone wall and the boy threw a golden ball over and beyond the wall. Of course, the children had to escape and go after their golden selves in the world. I haven't been able to find the book this fairy tale was in but I can recall the message.

The guides went on: "You see the world, the silver world out beyond Victoria, as a glistening glass and steel empire ready to erupt into fabulous sights and visions for the future. Your heart opens like a butterfly. The wealth you have been seeking will be more than represented in your hands. You will have the power to affect a change in the world."

And with all the encouragement from spirit, I made the move.

FATHER REDEEMER

"Father redeemer," I said as I rounded the corner from the kitchen to the living room. I had taken a brief moment to reflect as I got a glass of water, pondering the religious feeling of this meeting with the man I had been sitting across from.

"Yes, that seems to be my role," Wolf responded. I think it was said slightly ruefully, but maybe just an acknowledgment of his truth.

Now living in Toronto, I had been anticipating this meeting with Wolf for several weeks before my trip back to Vancouver for my nephew's wedding. I wanted desperately to see Wolf again, and when he agreed, I planned the visit to Victoria after the wedding, rather than joining my family on a trip to Tofino. While I met with Wolf, everyone else was donning wet suits to surf the waves of the West Coast.

We arranged to meet at his local coffee shop, although my preference was to meet him at his home. I wanted a more intimate setting where I could open my heart. But no, Wolf wanted to meet at the café. The weather gods were with me as I pulled into the parking lot behind his condo. He met me and we begin to walk together. Almost immediately the heavens opened.

"OK, you win," he said, and we walked back to his apartment. I sat on the sofa opposite him. I was never so appreciative of Victoria rain.

The meeting was a completion. It was the most important thing I did on my trip west. I had wanted to ask for his forgiveness, and he gave it. I still think fondly about him, but I don't feel guilty anymore.

The idea for this final meeting with Wolf had come to me in a meditation led by an online guru, Davidji, during a twenty-one-day online meditation adventure I was participating in. I knew I needed to do this.

Forgiveness was the theme of this day's guided meditation. I was led to choose a person I wanted to forgive. In the floating space of my mind, I thought "my mother" but that didn't feel right. I realized I needed to forgive myself. So, I acknowledged that I hadn't always been the daughter she wanted or needed me to be, and I forgave myself for that. I gave myself the freedom I needed to let go of the mother-daughter dynamic that had plagued me while she was alive. I hope it gave her soul the ability to forgive herself. I now see my mother as a person with her own missions to accomplish in the lives I had shared with her.

It then occurred to me that I needed to ask Wolf for forgiveness. I still felt guilty for hurting him, leaving him in the way I did. It also seemed an appropriate time. It was just past Rosh Hashanah but still close enough, a time when Jews ask forgiveness of the people they feel they've harmed over the year.

Our meeting was less fraught with recriminations and hurt feelings than the previous goodbye when I had left to fly off to Toronto earlier that summer. It was a powerful release. I still love the man. He doesn't really understand that, but I still feel the soul connection that I felt when we first began our relationship.

INVITATION TO FORGIVE

This man is someone I love in my soul. I know he was hurt. As much as I was hurt, he was hurt. There was pain regardless of how it ended. I needed to come back to love — because I love him in my soul. That is the healing power of forgiveness.

Q. Is there someone in your life you need to forgive? Or perhaps you need to forgive yourself for something you feel you did against your own self or someone else?

Sit quietly alone and put your hands on your heart. Breathe slowly and deeply. Inhale into your heart, let it expand, and as you exhale let yourself release all negative feelings. As you breathe in, allow the words "I forgive you" to fill your heart.

19

MYSTERY SOLVED

To know what you prefer, instead of humbly saying Amen to
what the world tells you you ought to prefer,
is to have kept your soul alive.

— Robert Louis Stevenson

MALE/FEMALE

In my new home in Toronto, I had trouble getting back into the rhythm of my writing. "Would my style be good enough? Did I really have enough to write about?" Etcetera, etcetera.

So, I sat to meditate each day, hoping something would break free of the logjam.

Jonas came through with the wisdom I needed to dispel my doubts: "OK, the struggle between male and female in you is coming to a crossroads. Allow yourself a confluence — the strength of the masculine aspect being in the world to support the female within. You have a deep-abiding female aspect — emotional, magnetic — a powerful female energy which you feel extremely protective of. The burden was always on you to keep this female under wraps. Your mother was terrified for you. Perhaps she saw you as vulnerable and naïve. She did not allow her own female energy to thrive and therefore could not support yours. And your father preferred to see you as a child. You often wonder why he became angry at you when you were around eight and nine years old."

"That scene about church comes to mind," I replied.

"Yes, you were being more defiant and more independent at that time. This raised his ire. So, as you walked along the path through teenhood to adulthood, you were at first very shy and withdrawn with boys, but had a pretty face that drew them to you. You were fearful of losing the male attention and love."

Jonas continued: "So now you see you recreated the attachment to daddy — in the relationship with Wolf— and have finally broken free by asserting your independence and then flying away — literally flying to another city to embrace a new life. Now you are working on your thesis for your book — not *looking for* the voice within but *allowing* the voice within to shine … and polishing it to a brilliant sparkly presentation."

TAKE YOUR POWER LIKE AN EMPRESS

Thinking about the power that spontaneously came out of me as a nine-year-old, a vision came to my mind.

A Chinese Empress speaks to me with great pride in her voice: "I sit on a throne carved with dragons and serpents. I wear a beautiful golden-yellow silk robe embroidered with peacocks and pheasants, garlands of flowers trailing along the borders. I am the Empress . I sit with the prowess of a goddess and the strength of a lion.

"I run the show — don't you know?!" she blasts. "My feet no

longer live as carriers of my body. My four servants carry me on my palanquin.

"The definition of defeat is not that you lose but that you *think* you lose," she pronounces. "Because I lost the functionality of my feet, that does not mean that I am defeated. It means that I sit in high places."

I love the surprise the empress ended her lesson with. The vision reminded me of a memory I had years ago. As I stepped up the stairs in my house, I had a flash of myself as a Chinese woman with bound feet.

The guides entered the conversation with their words: "Worship of any deities, gods or goddesses, is fruitless unless you engage with the qualities of their power and bring that into yourself, feel yourself as the deity with the power to motivate, to activate, to make for happenings of great circumstance for the betterment of humankind. Hold your truth.

"The work of the devil is in the mind, in the heart that has been crushed, bent in the feet that fall with anger. Tormented souls need to recline and to rest. Help yourself to some rest. You are tired, tired of running around to the beat beat beat of the drum of the outside world where you engage in this turmoil that makes bad things happen to yourself and others."

And so I realized that I had needed to rest after my trip instead of beating myself up for being unproductive.

And then the floodgates to spirit opened.

MYSTERY OF EGYPT SOLVED

After these words of empowerment, my guides began to speak to me as if I was now part of the group. I had graduated.

They chimed in: "One thing we want you to remember today is that you are one of us. We are a great power dynasty. We may not become famous in our lifetimes, but we are very important. The world depends on us and other cabals to heal the rifts between peoples."

As this flowed through me, I felt myself in spirit, strong and powerful, being part of the gang, Jim on one side of me, Jonas on the other.

They continued: "Once each one of us had gathered enough power within, we deemed it appropriate to incarnate on the earth plane again as deep-seated spiritual beings who could handle the vagaries of the world without losing our connection to spirit.

"Now, we want you to understand the lifetime you led with free status as the daughter of the pharaoh and as a priestess in the temple. You were exercising both spiritual and physical power within your being. There were many who were able to connect to the earth plane and maintain a connection to spirit. This is why you settled on the journey of learning about the corruption of power through incarnations, beginning with your first exile from Egypt with the Jews."

"Dipping your toe into the Jewish faith taught you the lesson that all people need community," Jonas explained.

"This is what I eventually came to realize about my parents' connection to the Church. They were not devoutly religious but they enjoyed being part of the community where they became friends with people who had families like ours," I responded.

Continuing on this thread: "Your time with the Jews — you were beginning to see how so many people were like little lambs that had no idea how powerful they were in spirit and so felt like they needed to follow a godlike figure through the desert. Through their own anxiety and fear, they needed that figurehead. You see, belief in a system joins people together in harmony. Like many, the Jews were afraid to lose their community as they moved to new locales. Moving from one location to another became a way of life that created the need for a cohesiveness as they struggled to survive.

"You did stay for a few years in that life but, realizing that your personal ability to connect with spirit was greater than your need for a father figure to be an intermediary between his people and spirit, you left that situation. You left the Jews, for you found you could not tolerate the menial tasks required of you as a woman. Within that patriarchal society, you could not teach the power of spirit to the people. That was the distinct purview of the elder men. The 'wandering in the desert' was not your idea of a pleasant time. The situation did not suit your educated, mystical mind. You snuck back to Egypt in the guise of someone else and began to teach the spiritual truths to those who supported you."

I had seen the vision of returning to Egypt before. The guides were confirming this, but what followed after this explanation was breathtaking.

Jonas continued: "You reconnected with the secret cabal, the bringers of understanding of the Universal Power. From the Spirit realm, you channeled the universal understanding through your crown chakra into your mental capacity, and the rock of the Earth grounded you. The kundalini energy that flowed through all your open chakras became the basis for your understanding of power in the world. Through many lifetimes, you have explored how the misuse of power, often male power against female, is a result of the blockages of different chakras. Changelings are now being born on Earth, including many boys who will grow into men who have acceptance of the female aspect within themselves. Therefore, they will not feel the need to have power over women in the way it has been exercised throughout history."

I had no problem visualizing myself in Egypt, sitting on the dry golden earth in a circle, meditating with my mystic friends. We were learning of our roles on the earth plane and knew we would be disseminating the message of the power of Spirit within. As I sat cross-legged, an image illuminated my mind. I saw a set of vertical glass towers reaching into the sky, gleaming gold in the sun. My towers in Vancouver ...... From the banks of the Nile, I was seeing into the future!

It was in that moment ... that magical moment suspended in time ... that I knew. I knew I was living where I was intended to, millennia later. I know who I am.

IT'S MAGIC

That vision changed the game board. I have transcended time to once again be one of the guides to help us recall that we are all spiritual beings experiencing human lives — not the other way around.

Jonas spoke to me of my mission: "The vision you saw of the future is why you had the courage through all the lifetimes you have lived to speak out, to link to the higher power, to link to the beautiful energy within and create a full picture of the dynamic of the soul on the earth plane. It was the challenge for the people of wisdom you associated with to go underground and draw from this wisdom again and again and again until the entire earth plane was permeated with people growing into wisdom individually. This is the time you have arrived at. It is the big puzzle that each one of you must recognize. The power is within."

Invitation to Link to Your Purpose

Years ago, I followed a guided meditation to discover my purpose in life. When I was working as an artist and designer, the answer at the time was to create beauty in the world. I have since realized that when a person recognizes beauty, they are seeing the presence of spirit. Now I am engaged in presenting spirit through the medium of writing. All is creative, all is an act of godliness.

Q. What are you divined to bring to the world? What is your purpose in life?

To help discern the answer, write out a list of things you love to do and include a list of all of your talents. Don't be modest! This list should give you clues. Read it to yourself, close your eyes, and ask yourself, "What is my purpose?"

Allow the answer to float into your mind.

OR

Use a writing prompt: "I have come into the world at this time to share my talents. The purpose is ......"

Perhaps you came to use your negotiating skills to bring peace to your family or others in the world.

Perhaps you came to guide others.

Perhaps you came to be a thought leader for a town or country.

Perhaps you came to experience the beauty of the world and share it with others.

Perhaps you came to be an example of the power of the physical body.

Perhaps you came to raise children of great wisdom to be themselves in the world.

Perhaps you came to be an agent of change.

Each person is unique in their talents and interests and has a gift to bring to the world.

III
STARSHIP

DREAM TIME

Much can be gained on Starship Earth
Playing with the monsters of the past
But more, more is the purpose, more.
The monsters of the past
Heat up the life's blood, the life's power
To project the positive growth
The positive purpose at hand.

Therefore
Plow under the past
Purport to be sorry
Which you truly are
But pilot yourself into pure love
Into pure stillness
Into pure purpose of soul's growth
And expansion into the more.

New purposes will blossom
New powers will explode on the scene
New blossoms will burst with scent of spring
And hopes and dreams of the past
Will be forgiven
For taking you on the path
That pained the heart
But salved the soul.

Tomorrow you will fling your rod and staff
To the gods
To the mind in the sky
To the momentous changes
In the world's eye
And burnish your own words
That make amends to no one
But portend for the power of the stars.

20

SHAKEN, NOT STIRRED

For truly we are all angels temporarily hiding as humans.
— Brian Weiss

WE COULD BE ANGELS

Spring had arrived on my nineteenth-floor balcony. A little sparrow fluttered under the railing to the deck that holds a banquet of bugs — tiny black specks that he gathered in his beak then dropped and gathered up again in a little ball to fly off and share with his mate. I would watch for him the next day.

As my angels and guides returned to me each day, I sat in my swan chair in front of my little altar and opened my mind to the flood of energy that the universal force provides. Words dropped into my mind — words from my angels, my divine spirit friends — for me to disperse.

"You could be Earth Angels discovering the bounty that awaits. The bounty of guidance, the bounty of supply, the bounty of wisdom that you so long have set aside and ignored. Tune up the vibration of your mind to the angelic realms and be a conduit for the treasure chest that is available to you. Be a channel for the wisdom, be an opening for peace, be the driving force towards happiness and fulfillment of dreams."

I expand on what my guides say: We are Earth Angels as we allow our spirits to move us through our lives and shine the divine light that is available to all through our talents and our love of the world around us.

Be you — not what others think you are but the angel you know you are. BE YOU.

MANY MESSAGES

I was treated to a cocktail of new stories from my spirit guides when I started listening to the online "21-Day Meet Your Spirit Guide Adventure" led by Sonia Choquette with Mike Dooley. I signed up for this program for the fun of it, and certainly my guides were having fun with me. They were activated, shaking it up, bringing in new understanding, introducing themselves in other lifetimes, leading me to shocking discoveries about my past.

I share the playful messages from spirit, some of them personal, some of them universal in nature, in hopes that others will realize we are all one in the universal power of Starship Earth. The universal adage "what you focus on, expands" is playing out in my life magnificently for my entertainment and enlightenment.

BRITBOX

"Oh, my goodness!" Guides were definitely popping in to let me know they were around. If I had any doubts that I was getting help with this book, the messages I received in this morning's medita-

tion would have dispelled them. A song ran through my mind …
"Chim Chim Cher-ee" from *Mary Poppins*. In the song, Dick Van
Dyke's character Bert asks the listener to blow him a kiss because it's
lucky. In the video I had watched just minutes before by the astrologer Bracha Goldsmith, she mentioned that when she does her daily
walks in Greece, a woman blows her kisses from a balcony.

"My goodness, of course we know what you are doing, ha ha," a
singsongy voice chirped.

She continued to give me directions to go for a nice long walk
today. She also commented about editors and how to proceed with
my writing for the coming week, all in the same voice of the British
shopkeeper from *The Indian Doctor*, the show I watched on the
BritBox streaming service last night. Double whammy! The guides
were obviously having some fun with me, telling me it's good to be
watching comedies.

"Just call us BritBox, and we will come around to brighten your
day." My shopkeeper added, "We want you to focus on the positive,
the joyful things that happened in your life as a child. This is very
important. Remember the wonderful walks you had with your father
in the woods filled with trilliums and dogtooth violets. You would
arrive home to look up the names of the little flowers you picked and
then press them in a book."

Then the voice of the doctor from the show told me, "You have
little butterflies flitting about your face — little pieces to insert into
the text you've already written — and above your head are your blue
jays. They are helping you with the organization of the book as well
as working on the book directly. The jays are also working to find
your people and pull them to your heart. You know that you have
connected with two very important people who responded to your

messages with phone calls yesterday. You have been in our thoughts for so long, to get you motivated to speak up. Now, Steve Harrison asked you a question in his Zoom webinar so that you spoke about your undertaking."

A few evenings before, I had participated in one of Steve Harrison's non-fiction book publicity webinars. I was surprised that it was live on Zoom, an opportunity for Steve to speak to participants about their book topics. When I saw my face in the line up at the top of the screen, I nervously thought, "Should I turn off the video — watch anonymously so I'm not picked to speak?" No, I bravely left my face up there. And, of course — he picked me first! So I talked about writing a book to expose the idea of past lives to a broad audience. He graciously listened. I also spoke with him by phone a few days later. I wasn't ready to participate in an extensive mentorship program, but the experience bolstered my confidence in sharing my thoughts with the outside world. "Wow, this was really happening!"

Jonas also expressed his enthusiasm, albeit in a British sort of way: "I say, well done, Lesley! Amen!"

The educated voice of Jonas continued with a lesson: "You know that the word 'amen' comes from Egypt. And you know it is related to Akhenaten, born with the name Amenhotep, who attempted to insert the idea of the one single god into the temples."

"The dictionary pins the etymology to early Jewish history."

"Well, did not the Jews live in Egypt for a time?"

And then, back to the Brits, "Your Noni brings in the British accent. Your Noni is part of this Choir of BritBox. Your Noni is having fun now."

"Is Noni still in spirit?"

"Not all souls remain for long before reincarnating. But the spirit of Noni is with Jim. Noni watched over Jim after he left the body. And Noni will be his spirit guide when he incarnates again into the family. Now, all is not written in stone as it was in ancient times."

An Old Friend Returns

A bright dot of orange flashed in my eye. I ignored it.

Another orange flash.

"OK … I'm listening," I said. "Oh, it's Wendy!" Wendy had come to me again after so many years.

Now, she continued as if to answer the query I had posed about her name long ago.

"Lesley, you do not know me from this lifetime. You know me from another time, another place, but we are dear friends. We are like twin souls. I do work with other people in your family, particularly your two nieces. You knew me in Egypt. We were sisters. We made people laugh. We were magic. We knew what was going on in the world, and we loved our world. You were the intellectual mind and could tell me all the stories of the world's enemies, truncheons, and treachery. I did warn you — I did warn you about that man, but you were so drawn to his power. You were drawn in by his magnetism. You could have been queen among the people if you had not been drawn in by him. But we understand the nature now of all the adventures you have explored. You have gone on a magical arc. The ark of the covenant."

"What? What do you mean?"

"The Ark of the Covenant is truly a representation of the connection to God's source which is within each of us."

After this revelatory reintroduction to Wendy, my new BFF, she carried on with directions for the order in which to clean up my condo in Toronto — such mundane things, but I receive instructions any time I stop and tune in for a second on what to do and when. Life happens step by step. Goals are attained step by step. So I'm appreciative of the guidance, and it frees my mind from anxiety — most of the time. One-two-three snap. It works.

"My job today ... Yes ... I hear ... My first job today is to tidy up my house." I laughed.

But before following these directions, I looked up the story of Peter Pan and Wendy. I discovered that the author James M. Barrie had based the characters on the children of his close friends.

The next morning as I prepared to meditate in my swiveling swan chair, the name Wendy kept repeating like a drill in my head.

Wendy, Wendy, Wendy ...

She greeted me as I sat.

"I did look up the family history after our last conversation," I said.

"You see, your mind takes you places to make connections. That is the female mind. It makes connections. I was indeed the Wendy in *Peter Pan*. The author of the book, J. M. Barrie, was a close friend of the family. He was a father figure to me, and I called him my 'friendy-wendy.' He was a wonderful writer and a wonderful man. So this is why I call my spirit-self Wendy. In spirit I have great wisdom which comes from ancient times, but I enjoy the fame of my persona from *Peter Pan*. Do not take me as a mere frivolous spirit. I am a female of great strength. You can call on me for anything related to women, for I am an icon in the minds of many — wink, wink, nudge, nudge. We work with what we've got, hey!"

She continued: "You have great ability to manipulate funds on the earth plane of your own accord, not to mention the assistance you are receiving. You need make amends to no one at this time. Take your time. Link to the higher powers. Bring in the energy of hope again. Your little winter pansies in the blue and violet colors have bounced back from the dusting of snow and are your hope for the spring that is around the corner.

"We are holding you accountable to being the female side of this big endeavor. For there is a need for the fluidity of thought that is brought through the female mind. So many writers have a formula — are formulaic. Of course, this is perfect for the topics they write about. But you have not got a 'topic.'"

"What? Then what do I have?"

"You have a force of will that works wonders. Notice the 'W's.'"

"You guides on the other side like to play with sounds, don't you?"

"Yes. It is punctuation. It is a way of drawing attention to the meaning behind the words. You, in life, tend to gloss over the surface of words. We use words in a way that requires interpretation. You, yourself, have been intrigued about the meaning behind words, their etymology, for quite some time. That comes from our influence on you, bringing new insights from ancient times, so that you see how the meaning has transformed through time. As you do this, you understand the misinterpretation of the words written centuries ago in what you call the Bible. Many scholars delve into the words as they are interpreted in different periods and expose how their meaning has been influenced by politics and the social realm of the time. That is why you are seeing treatises on the true meaning of the 'sacred' writings. And that is why there is such a fascination with finding original texts."

"I am beginning to hear Jonas's voice coming into this conversation," I interjected.

"Yes, he can be a bit pushy at times. After all, he is 'the wise man.'"
I smiled. I caught the hint of sarcastic fun in Wendy's voice. "But
let's continue," she said. "Now, most of these texts were written by
men during a long period of patriarchy. It is only now that this power
structure is beginning to break down."

I replied, "You know I take great umbrage at some of the texts
in the Jewish faith because they were written by men with deeply
misogynistic leanings — at least to my ear."

"Yes, this is true, for you have a need to update the understanding
of the nature of living on Earth which must — must, we say — incorporate the female outlook. And that is essentially what this book is
about."

"OK. Yes, I am so enthusiastic about the power of women's voices
today."

This conversation with my playful guide Wendy reminded me of
how my brain works when I'm writing and channeling my guides.
I come back to certain subjects again and again. It is like a spiral as
the ideas return to the same spot on a circle but on a higher level,
revealing more each time. A topic I discuss in one chapter may
take a turn to something entirely different the next time it comes
up. Many writers and artists believe that this is essentially how the
female mind works — like a mass of spaghetti connecting disparate
thoughts together. By contrast, men's brains can be compared to a
series of boxes. Many times, Wolf would say to me, "Would you get
to the point? You're driving me crazy!" His rational, scientific mind
wanted closure. The masculine, analytical left brain, if used exclusively, restricts new thoughts that may open new ways of seeing or
experiencing the world.

In our culture, we have leaned towards this masculine approach for so many centuries. Women, now entering into the world with power, are challenging this exclusive approach to life, are challenging the status quo. In general, women are said to be nurturing, more interested than men in consensus building. But I believe the differences go deeper than that. Women's brains are structured differently. There are more neuropathways between the two hemispheres of the brain in women which perhaps allows for more diverse ways of looking at a problem. Women use both the rational mind and intuition as a basis for action. Of course, these are generalizations and each person is individual.

Recently I had begun listening to a series of musical soundscapes with the app Synctuition. The soundscapes are specifically designed to create more neuropathways between the left and right brain which helps people become more open to their intuition. This is just one example of how people are using technology to connect more deeply with themselves, which in turn allows them to live more authentically in the world.

Throughout this life, my intuition has propelled me along a path of creativity. This path has enabled me to manifest a fulfilling life for myself. My ability to suspend rational thought for periods of time and drift into the universal mind has opened me to a world of inner experiences and wisdom. Each morning I sit cross-legged in my swan chair and eagerly await the new.

Jonas Reveals Himself

A multiplicity of sparkling white lights in my field of closed-eye vision gave way to an outline of two men walking together like the last scene of the classic movie *Casablanca*, when Bogart's Rick Blaine strolls off with Captain Louis Renault before the scene fades to black.

"Louis, I think this is the beginning of a beautiful friendship."

It was Jonas and next to him was ... Wolf! Such a surprise.

"What! Why haven't I seen this before?"

More is being revealed to me ... "Now, Jonas and Wolf are old friends — fellow travelers — Lesley. We have left this particular conversation till now for we knew that you would be tempted to stay with Wolf in Victoria if you knew how close he was with Jonas," my guides explained.

Jonas joined the conversation. "I was your priest in Egypt, Lesley. I knew you well."

Another shock!

"Of course I knew the trajectory you would be on. While I was training you as a priestess, we were well into your lessons for deep understanding of universal power and how to wield it in the world. I knew that you would go through the veils each time. In each lifetime, you progressed through understanding again. Those like you who were challenged in that Egyptian lifetime would return to share their knowledge. Your friends Emily and Bernadette were indeed two of those souls, and it was not a coincidence that you met them again in Victoria."

Thinking about Wolf, I added, "Wolf perhaps came back to challenge his rigid, judgmental, authoritarian way of being as a vizier and to connect with the spiritual aspects of his soul. I certainly challenged his judgmental nature."

"Now," Jonas continued, "yesterday you enjoyed the exercise that Sonia suggested during your online workshop. She asked each of you to imagine what type of dog you are when you are in your ego — your personality that operates in the world. This is a fun way to use metaphors to explain someone's personality."

"I said 'poodle, a standard.'" I saw myself as a black poodle named Priscilla, like the one owned by a friend of my grandmother whom I visited as a child. "Hmmm … What would Wolf be? … A poodle? No, a Russian wolfhound. But he always loved standard poodles — a beautiful white one named Khalil used to accompany him everywhere on campus when he was a professor. What does this say about me?" I wondered.

"Wolf was drawn to you because of your connection to spirit. You were a creature of creativity and mystery. Do you not know that it was me that prompted you to call Rob, who in turn invited you to that fateful lunch with Wolf?"

Jonas continued: "Now, I am working again with Wolf to plow his own fields. He has rows and rows and rows of poetic words written. Please encourage him to have these published."

The following day I sat to meditate ……

I saw an image of Jonas as the priest walking with Wolf, the pharaoh's vizier. He is telling the priest of my sexual indiscretions.

Jonas explained to me: "In addition to your sexual activities, you were part of the underground organization that was carrying on Akhenaten's practices and belief in one god. This would not stand in this country of many gods." This confirmed what I had imagined.

In my vision, Wolf continued with his dictates to the priest: "We must maintain the structure of the gods, the cadre of gods to which the people bow down. This is how we maintain our control over the lives of the many, so that they perform their roles within the structure of our society. The river gods of the Nile must be plied with caution as goods are transported along it. The fertility gods must inspire the planting of the seeds for growing grain — a reminder of the power of nature to urge the stockpiling of the granaries for feeding the armies.

The gods of war must be seen to maintain the men in their strength to fight for our empire. The god of the sun must be seen to maintain and inspire the workers to build upwards, towards the heavens. All must be maintained to keep the order of the kingdom. Therefore, this girl/woman may no longer reside with us, for she is a leader of people. She could create an uprising amongst the women, who ply their sexual trades for the pharaoh, and the children, who must speak in awe of the temple and the pharaoh. To maintain the structure of society, she must disappear."

Jonas added to me: "I sent you away. You know this to be true, Lesley. I sent you away. I needed to make it apparent to you that you must disappear and join the others. 'Leave. Leave the temple now! Do not look back! Run and join with those who are leaving. Do not look back. The gods demand it!'"

And I now recalled that he whispered in my ear, "But we will meet again."

"Our darling, you walked with Jesus, and you walked at the time of the story of Noah. You walked with Moses. You walked in the tradition created by the Jews."

All this gave me chills. I had opened myself to the guides. They did not disappoint. And there was still more to come.

21

ENCORE PERFORMANCE

*We would not open a pathway for you if you did not have what
it takes to accomplish it.*

— Jonas

THE BELLS SPEAK

Recently "Tubular Bells" repeated one morning as I lay in bed.
"Tubular bells … tubular bells." The message wouldn't let up until
I pulled up the album by Mike Oldfield on YouTube. I and a small
group of other spiritual people living on the Earth, whom I don't
personally know, are messengers selected and directed by a group of
spirits known as The Bells. The Bells, my spirit guides, are demanding
attention … I get it.

Inspiration! *Tubular Bells* — I could not turn the album off. I left
it on in the background as I listened to lesson three of the "21-Day
Meet Your Spirit Guide Adventure," in which Sonia talks about our
guardian angels — mine I have known for thirty-five years as Jonas.

"We wanted to remind you that The Bells are working with

you now that you have raised your vibration to a higher level. You only need to acknowledge their presence and thank them for their contribution."

Apparently my guides are sending me songs again, which, before I'd met them personally, would give me guidance for the day. Now they are prompts to dive in and connect to that massive energy field that opens like an ocean if I allow my mind to be still and simply let myself float. The world around me buzzes, hums, throbs with purposeful action towards the fulfillment of dreams. One must have dreams to open the joy of life — dreams of value, dreams of the heart's desire. The joy comes from the opening of the heart, and it plants a kiss on the face as a smile, a laugh, a wink of the eye.

The following day I was treated to more about The Bells. Many voices seemed to participate in my lesson: "You began your day after engaging with the Council of Higher Powers in your sleep, as you had requested before drifting off last night. The last thing you remember of your dream was something to do with horses and a foal just born. That's when you woke yourself up quickly. So, you see you are getting up on your feet as a foal does immediately after it is born — you will grow into the power force that you are. In the meantime, you will ride your white Pegasus through the sky, towards your Aquarian instrumentation of the final chapters of this book.

"Now, we want to speak a little more about The Bells. The Bells are of high spiritual standing within the Pantheon of what you call Heaven.

"The only name that represents us is 'a spirit group.' The Bells work as a call to action for those who have been chosen.

"You cannot say that we are angels. Many people understand that angels do *for* them, whereas we are requesting that *you do for us*. The concept of angels is an old one from biblical times of beings that bring essential ethics to the earth plane. At that time, a few were called to action, to activate understanding within the peoples of the world. But your earthly understanding of the Pantheon of Heaven through your religions ultimately changed to a belief that spirit has personality.

"Now, we, The Bells, have no personality, for there is no structure or need for personality. There is only the need for instilling the power of spirit of a high order to be instigated, activated on Earth. The instigation is for beings on Earth to recognize who and what they truly are — a magnificent manifestation through personality of the expression of spirit. As each person learns of their spirit guides, they see these as personalities likely from a lifetime they shared. These beings are all part of the Pantheon but have chosen to remain attached to those who are alive in body to assist in the direction of their understanding and, therefore, their activity in the world.

"There is no judgment from the Spirit realm placed upon your actions. All judgment that you may feel is self-generated from your own goals that you determined while in spirit — the pathway that you decided to execute before you entered the physical realm. All action on Earth has consequences. The consequences express to you whether you are on the right path for *you* or whether it is a divergence. If it is divergent and you recognize this, you will find a way to re-engage with the path that you set out on. These divergences expand the wisdom within — everyone diverges, for there is much temptation to play at activities on Earth. Lessons are learned that can be used on the path and moreover can be important for others to learn from. Therefore, the momentum that is created by actions reflected back by their results is important. This is called 'karma' and it does not mean 'punishment.'"

"OK," I understood.

The Bells: "We are biding our time. T. S. Eliot was activated by The Bells. Aleister Crowley — who devised the tarot deck you use — is of a different cabal but of the same level of wisdom. Aleister Crowley was steeped in the mystic arts from previous lifetimes that filtered down into his deck, which Frieda Harris painted. T. S. Eliot is like a wizard with blue, deep blue, and silver sky magic, and this is why you hold him in reverence.

"Our bond is with you. Purposeful action is required when you receive notification to do things. If it is a big thing, it'll take some time, so don't judge yourself.

"The wellspring of your understanding is deep. Your lifetime in Egypt prepared you for the misogyny, the fear of persecution, and it gave you the wisdom that all is not lost as the body is released and the spirit moves back into the universe of love. You are prepared for all eventualities, for the ability to escape pain by jumping out of your body, knowing that it is possible. Your lifetime in Egypt prepared you for the beauty, the spectacular beauty of the world and how spirit shines through with beauty. It prepared you for privilege. It prepared you with a sense of worthiness that underlies all your lifetimes despite where you came to in the end of each."

Twelve

I began to wonder more about The Bells. They had previously told me that there are twelve emissaries working for them on Earth at this time, one of them being me. This got me wondering about why twelve is such an important number. According to an article by Darlene Zagata, "the number 12 signifies perfection of government or rule. According to Bible scholars, 12 is the product of three, which signifies the divine, and four, which signifies the earthly." [1] The planets are also connected to the number since stars pass through the twelve signs of the zodiac, themselves representing twelve months in a year.

No wonder Jesus had twelve disciples. I am aware that I knew Jesus when he was alive. One of the students in a meditation class I led years ago was very close to Jesus in a past life and described her experience with him to me. Contemplating this as I got up from my swan chair and walked into my kitchen for a glass of water, my imagination kicked into play. I wondered, "*If* I was a disciple … what would my name have been?" In a flash, the answer was Peter. I looked up the name of the twelve disciples and there was Simon Peter. Hitting the highlighted link, I came upon a passage that stated "Peter was a fisherman and the son of Jonas."

Chills — chills ran through my entire body. "That's crazy!" Jonas had directed me to another lifetime in which I knew him. Still, I cannot presume that I was Peter in the time of Jesus. Perhaps Jonas was my father or at least a close friend to me. But it confirms that I did indeed know Jesus and Jonas during that period of history.

It was stunning to me how Jonas had led my mind to discover another lifetime when I knew him. The revelation had me wondering what would come up next. It then occurred to me that Jonas and I had a strong connection through religious experiences during many different time periods.

As if to confirm this, Jonas spoke: "Lesley, our soul connection is as strong as it is with your men Jim and Wolf. Each time we've been together, it has been in a spiritual context, understanding the deeper

---

1 Zagata, Darlene. "What Is the Meaning of the Number 12 in the Bible?" *Classroom*. 29 September 2017. https://classroom.synonym.com/what-is-the-meaning-of-the-number-12-in-the-bible-12085081.html

message behind the structure of the religious organizations of the era. Always it has been the understanding that all of us are divine. We all have within ourselves the power of the light. This has been our message. You are now writing to put it in the context of the twenty-first century. Why else do you think we direct you to this webinar by Sonia about spirit guides?"

"Oh, thank you! ... Jonas, do you have anything to tell me about Wolf and Jesus?" I asked.

"Yes. Wolf lived around that time, knew me and the twelve disciples, or at least Simon Peter, but he did not become a believer. He was a skeptic, for, as he explained to you, there were several men who purported to be the Messiah at that time. He was not inclined to take on any of them in their guidance."

I added, "He still holds it to be true that there were many who claimed to be the Messiah. I don't think Jesus actually claimed to be the Messiah. To paraphrase Jesus's message, he said, 'I am but a man among you. All that I can do, so can you.'"

I thought to myself, "OK ... perhaps Wolf was a priest or a leader of some sort in the temple." This made sense to me. "He was afraid that his power would be usurped by the power that Jesus wielded with his followers. It was the same fear that the priests felt in Egypt when Akhenaten tried to dictate that they all pray to one god. There is a strong connection there. It is about power over the people. Jesus was telling the people that they had the power within — this would take away the power of the priests just as Akhenaten's dictate would reduce the power of the priests by requiring them to relinquish their individual gods ... OK ... My goodness," I said. "It's all about masculine power."

As I've experienced in several of my past lives, the power I had gained as a woman through intuition and development of spiritual understanding was often thwarted by the patriarchal status quo of the time. Throughout history, men, striving for power, have perverted the original spiritual messages to suit their own desires.

One biblical story that could have been altered to suit the patriarchy is the story of the virgin birth. This never sat right with me. I speculate that Mary could have been a virgin in the temple, gifted by her family as a prestigious offer in respect of God. It is not inconceivable that she was secretly impregnated by an earthly man against the dictates of the temple rules. I know other women in history who got up to mischief!

There are many today who are interested in revealing the true complexity of the life of Jesus. Scholars like Elaine Pagels, whose work is based on the papyrus texts discovered in 1945 (named the Nag Hammadi texts after the location in which they were found in Egypt), delve into the history of early Christianity. In turn, their work has influenced writers like Dan Brown, whose popular series of books, which includes *The Da Vinci Code*, draw their basis from these texts. Other writers have channeled alternate histories of the stories and people that are presented to us as truth by our religious organizations.

Years ago, I read many treatises on the life of Jesus — *The Aquarian Gospel of Jesus Christ*, a channeled book, and *The Gnostic Gospels* by Elaine Pagels. I do remember a few of the details. Jesus was part of a group called the Essenes, a high-level mystical group of the Jewish faith that was active around the first and second centuries AD. I do have a sense that Jesus treated men and women equally, that the early Gnostics gathered both men and women in their ceremonies, each taking turn as leader. It was truly democratic. Jesus was a living example to humanity of the power that resides within each one of us.

22

STARSHIP EARTH

Live the full life of the mind, exhilarated by new ideas,
intoxicated by the Romance of the unusual.

— **Ernest Hemingway**

ANGELS, ARCHANGELS, AND ALL THE COMPANY OF HEAVEN
Before falling asleep one night, I sent a message to my guides that I wanted to connect with the Council of Wise Ones. I wanted to tap into higher understanding as I slept. My request was granted. As I sat to meditate the next morning, messages spilled down into my mind that seemed to be lessons for all of us earthlings, not just specific to me.

"You work daily with the Council of Wise Ones, all being alerted to your needs and the needs of the world. Our presence is becoming known. Challenges are great and manifold" — something I am often told by my guides — "for all of humanity now."

"Balance of power, balance of light" — also a phrase I am told regularly.

These are words that often come to me to begin my mediations — "Be alert to the changes."

The guides: "The healing of the planet is a cosmic event no longer in your control. The Earth has taken it upon itself to work the magic necessary to create the change in those who are stuck in the mud of immovability. Movement forward is required. The major disasters you see on Earth are in your faces now, for the little events have not budged the recalcitrant from their seemingly calm and settled lives.

"Worldly ambitions need to be broken down into smaller pieces for individuals to take up the cause. You can no longer expect others to propel you forward. Each person must learn to bend their will to no one and dance to their own drum. Waking up. Wake up. The angels are moving through the cracks and are available to all. Once you all are enveloped in the words of wisdom and the arms of love, we guides will cheer you on to your new paths of righteousness."

The guides qualified the meaning of the word that seems archaic in our world: "'Righteousness' meaning 'righting the wrongs' — not the kind of things your churches purport to be evil, sinful acts, but the righteousness of healing the Earth and caring for others regardless of who they are.

"We have a job to do, Lesley, and you have a job to do. Our job has always been to inspire you to create something beautiful that the world can see, that harkens to the sweetness of life.

"Whence you come so you go. Hope springs eternal. We can go on with all the homilies we frequently send to you, but our wish is for others who turn their faces to the sun, hoping for healing, to open their minds to the knowledge that they are loved and guided every moment of their days.

"Whence you come so you go. Turn up the volume from whence

you come and allow yourselves to walk the path of love and care for your planet and all people.

"Whence you come so you go. You know you will find heaven in the identical place that you walk now if you engage with the higher realms in your lives. Heaven is with you, is around you. It is the beauty that shines through every living thing. The Earth is pulsing. The Earth is having a heart attack right now from the stress it's been subjected to by the mindlessness of activity. Pray. See the light in everything. Meditate. Love the light in everything. Purport to know the difference between mindfulness and unconscious action.

"Whence you come so you go. Many are leaving the planet at this time due to the scourge released into the air by who-knows-who — it doesn't matter. It is a contagion of the mind. The wind spirits blow through the mind to clear it. Those who are not willing to be cleared of their mind's detritus breathe in their medicine to leave the planet and will look at their lives and their thoughts in a new realm. Analysis of your own thinking is what is required. 'Why have I not done what I said I would do? Why am I so reluctant to make the changes I say I want to? What is stopping me?' All these questions need answers. Those people unwilling to answer their questions are finding their escape routes.

"Whence you come so you go. Work with the minds of others. Many lightworkers have entered the planet recently. Much is to be said for listening to those with new ideas. We speak now of politics. 'All at once' is not too much for some, but there is a need to slow down when approaching change and allow others to catch up. Large groups are congealing and forming around new ideas. The wealth of nations depends upon this. No longer can countries hold on to their borders in order to demonstrate their power over other countries.

Cooperation is required in many areas. Let go of the need for the ego of country and become agents of change for the world.

"Whence you come so you go. 'Power to the People' was the rallying cry for change in the sixties. Let it again be the mantra. People, not countries, are what create healing on the planet. Cooperation, not perpetuation of power brokers. Be like Perceval, of Arthurian legend, who was given a glimpse of the Holy Grail. Childlike in character, protected from worldly temptation, he became known as a simple hero. The heavens open for all who care to allow themselves to be present in the moment and hold their own lives as they would a baby, with love and serenity, knowing that all is well and will be. World without end. Amen."

Whence you come so you go.

Get off the merry-go-round and get onto the Ferris wheel.

STARSHIP

"Starship Earth. We call it 'Starship' because it is the planet for learning to be the star that you are. The challenges may be great and manifold but they are worth accomplishing towards your goal of being your true self. Everyone on Earth at this time is presented with options to transform themselves in some way. The cosmos is opening up the energy for this transformation. In each moment throughout history there is a movement forward that's available for each individual. There is a *critical mass* happening now in which many people are waking up to their potential, to the matter at hand, to find ways to connect to their true selves and connect to others without prejudice. That is truly the goal — the highest goal of the Aquarian Age — the acceptance of the individual with their unique qualities within the whole of humanity. Band of brothers, band of sisters , but with a difference."

Warp speed ahead. Make it happen.

GENERATIONAL ZEITGEIST

French political philosopher Alexis de Tocqueville wrote eloquently about the changing of the generations: "Among democratic nations, each generation is a new people. And those generations are defined not by age or by family relationships, but the major historical and social events of their lifetimes."

Jonas and my guides expanded on this idea in today's world: "The generation after (the chaos of) World War II created a stable and structured society in which they moved humanity forward and encouraged their children to think for themselves. They created a platform for the burgeoning forth of the baby boomer generation which has moved out in the world with greater freedom of thought and the ability to make changes in the conceptual life."

To this conversation I added: "I have always thought that the Beatles were activators of a wave of transformation in the twentieth century. They played a magnificent role in bringing Eastern philosophy to the West — Ravi Shankar, transcendental meditation, and the breakdown of organized religion. They were living their talent and fulfilling a philosophical shift required in the world."

The guides went on: "The boomers, in turn, have brought forth children with even greater freedom of mind and intellect who are continuing to create an atmosphere of higher mind and peace, beauty and harmony, in their own enjoyment of life, in their pleasure in the sweetness, in their lavish love of the world's beauty. They, in turn, are bringing forth another new generation of wise children with depth of purpose to be born on the earth plane at this time.

"Now, the newer generations — millennials and Gen Zers —

for the most part have not experienced the horrors of the early- to mid-twentieth century as you have. Some have no idea what cataclysmic events needed to occur to create the world they live in now, to create the prosperity, the wealth of nations. They have a cleaner slate to work from. Many have reincarnated with the memory of the Renaissance. It's not that they have not experienced hardship, but they do not have a heavy burden like that instilled in the boomer souls who quickly reincarnated during or just after or World War II.

"Generations have limits but also talents. Large swaths of energy emerge from each generation with a theme that has been called for on Earth and is taken up by the majority of souls entering the earth plane at a particular time. Millennials have so much enthusiasm and hope that their desires will be fulfilled. They don't have the fear of losing their privacy. They are the leading edge of universalism — of the ability to speak their mind without fear."

"Although that freedom may be backfiring at this time in the politics of the US," I added to this discussion.

"We all play a role in the march of history," the guides continued, "sometimes as citizens in a country living out a very private karma within the huge movement in the evolution of humankind. Sometimes we play a major role on the world stage, in the greater sweep of philosophy that lives in the heart as an underlying theme to each in our daily lives. People of the world are propelled to fulfill themselves. Individuals are propelled to fulfill their talents, to fulfill their God-given rights in whatever they deem is the best opportunity for them."

Wake up to your time! Feel the very personal purpose of your life but also hear the strains of music playing for your generation. Humanity awakens instant by instant. Each small moment is a momentous change in the world, the universe. Power to the People, Girl Power, make the world whole again. These are breezes and eddies of the wind that blows through our history, seeping into every cell of our bodies as we take our deep breaths in yoga classes, in daily meditations, making a meal, sitting in the hair salon, taking the dog for a walk. The whispers of the OHMs, Shreem Brzee, Sweetness of Life — we reap the benefits of the collective sounds and the collective joyous arias. Make it yours.

Deepen your field of love by deepening your breath and the vision in your mind's eye. Love your neighbor as yourself. Live life as if this is it. Because it is. THIS IS IT.

Every moment is my moment. Every moment is your moment. Make it IT.

WE ARE ALL SOULS

We are all souls

Donning our many disguises

We all get down

To the successes and failures

Which have propelled us forward

Each in our own destinies

In our own successful flowering

To hold our faces to the sun

And be grateful unto thee.

Wherefore art thou?

GEMS OF TIME

The grand piano plays softly
As we speak of the burgeoning forth
Of the children
Of the flight of the doves around the bend
In the world's eye
Wink, wink, nudge, nudge
Is it all just a joke
Is it all just a play
To dissolve into nothingness?

No, it is electrified
Electric channels of light
We fly through these channels
To draw you along
To allow the fog to drift away and let you peek
At the orchestra playing
In the field of your past dreams.

Smooth over the ruffles
Smooth over the weeds
Let them become the fodder, fertilization
Of the beauty of the rows
Of she who opens the bud in the wink of an eye
And sends her petals to the sky
Petals of pink and petals of green
Petals of mauve, all to be seen
For the beauty in the eye of the beholder.
We draw the eye down mystical lanes
Of magic purported to be in vain

STARSHIP EARTH

But all is well when well is enough
To propel the soul
To make more memories
Of hope and dream
The delight in the eye of the beholder
Of the representation
Presented in your world
Is often more than you can bare.

Your words ring out
Notice those who care
And those who don't get in your hair
And mess around and tune you up
But you will never be bare enough
In the world
To share the magic of the light
You can only hope or swear
Whichever you choose
To make amends or make love
Whichever you choose
To conquer the ills
And hold your head high.
Forthwith thou must repare
To a glade within the wood
Where all must be alerted
To all that has been good
And whence you come to such a place
Thou must remember
You are in grace.

23

STARSHIP ESSENTIALS

Star light, star bright,
First star I see tonight,
I wish I may, I wish I might,
Have this wish I wish tonight.

— **English language nursery rhyme**

STAR BRIGHT

Beginning a new day, I sat down in my swan chair to meditate. I pulled a tarot card, the Star — a lovely swirling image of a woman water bearer. She holds up a vessel of water that spills from a star-studded, deep purple and pink sky down to a crystal-strewn earth. Of course — Aquarius, representing inspiration, crystallization, self-recognition, connection to universal intelligence. I glanced at the sparkling rings on my altar desk, picked up a pinky ring with diamonds set in a star-like rosette, and put it on my right hand. Perfect. I crossed my legs in the chair and settled comfortably to begin to raise my vibration by chanting. I let go of all thought, and I opened to a higher field of energy, far above planet Earth. A vision formed in my mind.

"Wow, I am seeing an energetic layer around the Earth, beyond the atmosphere. I am floating in a field of peace. It is our universe, filled with our planets and stars. It is a purple energy that permeates from beyond gravitational force into the Earth's atmosphere and activates the energies within the cells of humans. All is connected."

The guides acknowledged: "OK, you're only now becoming aware of how much the stars and planets create an atmosphere for particular development on the earth plane. The Earth is alive, the air is alive. The energies created on the Earth project outward. There is a barrier, at the edge of the atmosphere, that bounces back at you the violence and aggression that you have created. Now, when you raise your mind above the atmosphere of the Earth into the higher planes, you can receive higher understanding.

"You are seeing that the wind, the rain, the fire are activated on the earth plane, creating floods, hurricanes, earthquakes, tornadoes. This is the Earth responding to the upheavals in human relations. The Earth is cleaning up its systems just as you detoxify your body with herbs, trying to create a smooth flow within your body. So the Earth wants to flow again, moving through the crust of toxicity created by the emotions and garbage of humankind. The work has begun. The Earth is forcing humankind, alerting humankind to move beyond. All shifting energies create dynamic forces. Some people react negatively to the need for change, clinging on to the old belief systems that create toxic emotions within the body, just as old belief structures within the planetary consciousness create animosity between peoples.

"Now, all who are attempting to understand their own natures on a deeper level are moving towards the cleansing of the Earth, the renewal of the glory of the universal energy sprouting up all over the world.

"Science will be the savior of the world. The proponents of scientific truths are letting people in on the secrets. They will be broadcasting the new paradigm of the Age of Aquarius, ready to move forward. If scientists and engineers can build a tunnel under the Alps, the world can responsibly respond to the need for clean energy.

"Many more women are going to need to be drawn into the sciences. The energy of the planet is shifting. There is a bounty of intellect in the world that is unfettered, and once the minds are set to a task, humanity will be propelled forward."

INVOCATION —
IT IS TIME FOR YOU TO INVOKE THE RETURN OF THE WISE ONES.
The guides continued: "We want to speak about the yearlings, the young ones who are entering now and those who will be entering soon. You are creating the platform for their intelligence, their brilliant new minds and creativity coming in from the higher plane. Those on Earth who are praying for peace, for love, for light are energizing the souls of these young newcomers and are holding them dear to their hearts. These yearlings, as we will call them, are responding to the need for a renewal of ideas, renewal of a way to behave on Earth so all people are respected with understanding, with caring. This does not take away the responsibility of the individual. You can no longer project your troubles outward onto others. Resolution comes about by looking within. This is a central core of the new Earth rising — personal responsibility.

"Now, of course, what will we do with the boys? Testosterone creates a need for using the body with aggression in both males and females. Your sports, your games use the energy of aggression without harm. They are a celebration of the body and mind in harmony. The Olympics were created as a celebration of aggression used creatively. They are perfect examples to set the world on a path of retreat from wars. One must understand that the play is within the mind. The adrenaline floods the body and needs a release. The truth is that all sides win when aggression does not harm, does not boil over into war.

"Much has been written about the causes of the First and Second World Wars, the Vietnam War, and the wars in the Middle East and Afghanistan. All of this has been written about, actions and reactions on a human, three-dimensional level. We want it to be viewed from a higher plane of understanding. As the yearlings, the new young ones, begin their trek on Earth, you will see a new era of peace being ushered in. A new Earth!

"You are being asked to write this book. You have been directed by us guides for many centuries in the guise of many different personalities. You are being directed to speak to those who are just beginning their quest for understanding. You are being directed to help the process of integration for the young ones to come in. You are being directed for the purpose of assisting others to ignite the sparks of light, ignite the stardust within the mind.

"Do you know that silica is an activator of the pineal gland, which is the spiritual receiver in the brain? Silica is a component of sand, and we speak of the sands of time. Spark the stardust within the brain. The stardust in the background of your mind is the history of humanity, of all that has been and all that will be."

New Day Dawns

A new day dawned. Wind swept across the glass panes of my nineteenth-floor balcony railings, rattling me awake. I began this day with a sense of unease. I wasn't sure where to start on the plan for the week ahead. It was a new moon the night before, and I should have good intentions for the new lunar beginning.

My horoscope on the Co–Star app said: "Your heart is an ocean liner sailing on stormy seas."

"Well, that fits my mood." Scanning the internet, a sinking feeling of jealousy began to fill my heart. This was not a new feeling, and even now, after all the soul-searching and guidance, it rears its ugly head at times. I needed some relief from this nagging that seemed to float in the back of my mind and subvert my intentions. Getting closer to the end of this project, I began to compare myself to the success of others and found myself coming up short. I wished that I had spoken out earlier in my life. I would normally just pull myself together and, as the British saying goes, "keep calm and carry on." But today I wanted clarity.

I sat at my table with all the golden power icons I placed there and lay out the question.

I asked my guides how to resolve the feelings of jealousy I often contend with. I know we shouldn't compare ourselves to others, but that is sometimes hard to remember in this competitive world. "At what age did this begin?" I asked. "It has left me feeling that I could not achieve the highest success I have aimed for in life."

Immediately I heard that it was at age five. The spirits outlined all the circumstances, little betrayals and slights, involving family, friends, and neighbors from that time of my life. It goes back that far. They then told me that it is a continuation of a pattern in my mother's family.

And so it goes through families until the hour glass is turned upside down and a new path begins ......

To encourage me, my guides send me a poem:

OUR STARSHIP

The sands of time
Filter through the rocks
And are washed clean by the ocean air
And the salt of the sea.
To see beyond the works on earth
To make for new again
And behave in patterns of power
Unto god of the universal force.

The hopes and dreams
For the future of humanity
Begin to be fulfilled
As the sands are cleansed
And blow through the air,
Whip up the ideas of new propensities
And propose the peace
That will walk upon the earth
If taken to the heart.

It is a matter of knowing
Every day
That you are loved
That challenges are only directives back
To your true value

STARSHIP ESSENTIALS

As a being of god on the earth
The flowering of humanity is beginning again
The flowering of love potions
Float on the air waves
And purport to be signs
Signposts for the coming
Of the wellness
That truly is forgiveness of all
And forbearance of all
That is not in alignment
With this truth.

More souls are rubbing
The sleep from their eyes
And seeing the true value
Of their walk upon the earth
All begins in the Now
All begins in the heart of hearts
All bows down to no one
All riches are within
Peace be still.
Rest in your own calm
It is within your heart
To love yourself
And be no one's pawn
On the game board of life.

And so …… we carry on.

Starship Essentials

A new lesson came from the guides: "Starship Earth. The Earth wants to be appreciated just as you do. The Earth is willing to give of its bounty if it is appreciated. The animals are willing to give of their bodies if they are appreciated. They know their place in evolution. They know it is time for them to be loved again. There is more to be said regarding loving the animals than you can see with your eyes. So many younger souls — younger in age and often younger in soul development — crave the touch and essence of animals. For the animals live their essence, and they know what they are here to be and do. They each do have personality, particularly those animals with higher brain power. Those that have been given the task of living with humans know their role in the human's life.

"You are well aware of your cat's essence as a female who enjoys the pleasure of being petted and touched and massaged and told how beautiful she is. She sees your energy and responds as she wishes. She also sees other energies. You became aware of this when you first moved into this condo. You noticed she seemed to be responding not just to the unfamiliarity of the location but to the residual energy of the place.

"The birds you see on your walk are well aware of the energy you send to them. They see you with ultra-vision, with energy beyond what the human eye can see. So do cats. Dogs are more earthy but are evolving more into playthings, away from the carnivorous beasts they began as. Birds in cages are aware of their sacrifice and hold their owners to account. All animals will behave in manners to make humans pay attention to them. If they are not able to live their essence, their stress hormones cause them to issue distressful behavior.

"You all on the earth plane have a seat on Starship Earth. What you do with that seat is important. What each person does with the animals is extremely important. There is a great wave of love flowing around the Earth that holds the animals dear. Often it is the animals, their plights, that take people to parts of the world that they would never encounter otherwise, where they learn of other people's lives, understand, and move mountains for change. This is one of the ways animals help the planetary healing process.

"The planet has not forgotten its own needs and so it shows humans their folly — their folly in not respecting it.

"Now, many people are taking off their collars and are speaking out — becoming free to be in their essence — to be powerful against their masters. You are one of these people. You have a big personality when you begin to speak, when you feel free to hold yourself accountable to be true to your essence."

FLOWER POWER

"Is it not a miracle that a flower bud opens its petals to the sun to hold itself in pure beauty in obeisance of its true nature?" I mused as I marveled at the infinite forms of God in our world.

As I opened my mind to the guidance in my morning meditation, I heard: "Our darling, you need to balance your energy. Pay attention to your solar plexus." Realizing I wasn't breathing through it, I let my body relax and allowed my breathing to flow more smoothly, imagining the expansion of the sunlight color activated in this chakra.

In my mind's eye, I found myself lying on a comfortable bed, looking up into the most luminous lemon-yellow created by the sun's light as it filtered through a cloud of yellow petals. "Oh, I am in a healing center," I realized, a place with rooms filled with the colors of the chakras magnificently activated by masses of flowers, each healing room with one color to bathe the body in energy — healing garden rooms.

"This is a spa of the future that uses color therapy, the transfer of color through the plant structure," my healing guide explained. "It mystically opens the mind and body to the alchemical process of turning light energy into matter. A flower begins as a tiny seed, grows into a beautiful green structure, then a small bud expands and opens into an explosion of color. This is the same process as the cells of your body, which open to the magic of energy from the sun, from the air, and from the cells of the structures you ingest. As you bathe in the nature around you, you become aware that all things are expressions of life. You wake up to the reality that energy is within everything on the planet."

This was an incredible experience of potential future spa centers. It was a thrilling look into the future.

My guides continued: "These centers draw upon the natural ability of the Earth to heal and of the body to heal itself. The work is just beginning to bring the Earth back into harmony. Ultimate healing from fluorocarbons and CO_2 in the air on the earth plane will be maintained by a global consortium of companies loading up all the carbon into bins to recreate more matter of import and manufacture. Chemistry and physics combine in the new world to bring about the fruition of humanity's cooperative ventures *with* nature rather than by using nature. Engineers are working on this. The Earth will be a source of pleasure and enjoyment, butterflies and birds will abound again. Power is in the hands of concerned people. Power is in the hands of those donating their days to this cause. Cooperation between the masses of peoples will require governments that focus on the future of power for and of the people — to activate power, to engage power, to inspire power, to motivate power.

"You are part of the motivation segment of humanity. Creativity is a motivation that comes from the source of God's energy flowing through you. This book will be finished, and as you continue your journey down the River Nile, metaphorically speaking, you are picking up more exciting visions of future."

The guides suggested: "The world's most brilliant gardeners and architects may well be on the forefront of the truth that the healing of the Earth entails a cooperation between the Earth and humankind in recognition of God's gift that was given in love."

AQUARIAN ARCHITECTURE

As I pondered the future of our planet, I thought, "Engineers can send rockets to the moon and Mars, so they can surely build an apartment tower that draws its energy from the Earth and the wind and the life-giving sun."

Deep in a meditation, I saw a vision of a new type of city — one that is respectful of the natural landscape while still fulfilling the needs of its inhabitants. Condo towers rise up from the ground as central poles, leaving the surrounding land below free for nature to flourish, animals to roam without fear of human interference. Platforms of residences project above ground off the poles in layers, leaving spaces between to plant gardens on the roofs, to grow food and flowers and support the animals that thrive with humans. The energy of the sun is drawn through the interior to the back of each apartment with reflective mirrors, creating power for each apartment and adding to the core to power the entire building's structure.

The guides spoke further about the future: "Yes, you are correct.

There is and will be a world of highly developed creative architects, engineers, and designers who transform the way people live and work in order to respect this beautiful planet. You are granting yourself visions of a new world of architecture with many new types of living situations. You are already seeing, in Dubai and other places in the world, architectural feats that have challenged the world to change its contours."

The next day, I added, "I'm also seeing buildings that look like giant mushrooms dotting the landscape."

"Yes, these are just a few design ideas that will be options in the future."

This was a new and exciting development — looking forward instead of back, viewing the creative works of future generations. With my meditations taking me into the future, the designer in me enjoyed the playful visions. I began to wonder what would happen to the offices left empty as the work force would change its needs after the Covid-19 pandemic. Many people have been required to work from home and some may choose to continue to do so, if only part of the time. Can office towers be retrofitted? Can they become homes in the sky? Can you knock out windows to create recessed outdoor spaces? Can you eliminate every other floor to create room for energy collection at the ceiling level, in line with new environmental policy? Can you maintain the integrity of the structure while making such changes? I was quite enamored with these ideas and told a friend about them.

He said, "There is one problem with this picture — where to find enough of the precious metals and other materials to manufacture the chips for the new technologies."

"Well," I said, "I heard that there are lots of minerals floating around in asteroid fields in space." "Exploration of space?" I think — I keep this to myself. I am not a scientist and know that my ideas sound a bit wacky! That's my futurist Aquarian mind. But it is fun to speculate about what could be possible in the future.

TOWERS OF LIGHT THEN AND NOW

The old skins become new as new skin becomes old.
We work our magic. All possibilities.

— Jonas

"Speaking of modern architecture, how can it be possible that I viewed the towers of the future from my past — far back in ancient Egypt?" I asked Jonas in meditation.

"Words represent the ideas of people through time," he explained. "The towers of light represent structure through time. The science within the mind is flung into the future and therefore, just as you have seen the possibility of different types of buildings a century into the future from your present time, so could you see, in your mind's eye, shimmering glass towers while sitting cross-legged in the sand on the banks of the Nile, in the shadow of the pyramids. Just as the face carved on the Sphinx was updated from the original lion's head, so can you extrapolate from one form to another in the future."

"That makes sense," I replied. "I imagine this relates to the concept that all time exists at once — a concept, by the way, that I still can't get my head around."

"That is not necessary, as you are able to travel in your mind to understand yourself in other timeframes and within the life forces around you now.

"Now," Jonas suggested, "let us work our magic today with your words."

Now
The Great Lake peers up at me from between the two towers and broadens out to the expanse of the southern horizon. A pair of swans — my swans — which only yesterday floated on a far lagoon, have made their way through the waterways to grace my first survey of the world from my nineteenth floor.

Below me, a parade of dogs leading their wards along the pathway that borders the lagoon brings a smile to my lips. I have figured that French bulldogs are the breed du jour by my unscientific survey. Next come the doodles and unspecified breeds, large and small, from unknown places, their owners themselves a mix of peoples from all over the world.

Gentle ripples of lake blue sparkle and dance on windows to the music of construction and back-up beeps.

The outline of Toronto, the city of my youth, etches the sky to the east.

"How did I get here?" I wonder at the move I recently made after nearly forty years of living on the West Coast. But I know I am in the right place ... for now.

And yet ... another horizon beckons ... and this one has palm trees.

ABOUT THE AUTHOR

Lesley Corte is a gifted psychic visionary, spiritual teacher, artist, and writer. Her strong spiritual and psychic abilities were revealed early in her life during classes with a brilliant psychic named Kitty Massey. She met her main spirit guide at this time and, with his tutelage, began to lead classes herself in spiritual development, meditation, past life regression, channeling, and chakra energizing as well as participating in large psychic fairs.

As a deep thinker and seeker, Lesley's intuitive development began at Sir George Williams University, where she received a Bachelor of Fine Arts degree. She continued into the field of graphic design, using visions that would present themselves to her to create solutions for her work. She then moved into event design, where she executed visions of beauty and excitement for corporate events in high-end hotel ballrooms. Throughout this time, she continued to do psychic readings and lead meditation groups as well as explore her own past lives. The understanding she gained of her own soul's development and path through history seemed an important discovery that she was propelled to share, resulting in the creation of this book.

Today, Lesley enjoys spending part of her year in the tropical country of Panama, living in her beach condo overlooking a palm-tree-lined bay of the Pacific Ocean.

Facebook

www.facebook.com/people/Lesley-Corte/100063827688469/

Instagram

www.instagram.com/lesleycorte/

Website

www.lesleycorte.com

LinkedIn

www.linkedin.com/in/lesley-corte-0045b8289